THE WORLD OF SILENT FLIGHT

From time immemorial people have wanted
to fly. For centuries getting a kite in the air
was as close as they could come...

... Flight is only two hundred years old. ... Ballooning, one of man's earliest successes in the air, was the marvel of the 18th century ...

... Once man got started he outflew the birds. He's just as silent but he can glide faster, higher, further and do aerobatics ...

... If it's a charge you want, there is nothing more exciting than jumping ...

. . . Finally, with only a wing on his back, man has learned low, slow flight and now emulates the birds.

THE WORLD
OF SILENT
FLIGHT

Richard A. Wolters

McGRAW-HILL BOOK COMPANY

**NEW YORK · ST. LOUIS · SAN FRANCISCO · DÜSSELDORF
LONDON · MEXICO · SYDNEY · TORONTO**

Other books by the author:

THE ART AND TECHNIQUE OF
SOARING
ONCE UPON A THERMAL
GUN DOG
WATER DOG
FAMILY DOG
CITY DOG
KID'S DOG
INSTANT DOG
BEAU
LIVING ON WHEELS

All photographs by Richard A. Wolters except:
John DesJardins, pages 23, 39, 40, 41, 57
Edward Hanke, 73, 77, 78, 79, 80, 81, 82, 83, 96
George Uvegas, 123
Pat Rogers, 151, 172, 173, 176 right, 177
Ernst Liniger, 176 left, 180
Swiss National Tourist Office, 179
From the collection of the British Museum, 3, 4, 5
From the collection of the New York Public Library, 11, 25, 26, 27, 64
From the collection of Go Fly A Kite, 6, 7, 10, 15

34567890 HDHD 8543210

LIBRARY OF CONGRESS CATALOGING IN PUBLICATION DATA
Wolters, Richard A
  The world of silent flight.
  Includes index.
  1. Gliding and soaring. 2. Balloons. 3. Parachut-
ing. 4. Kites. I. Title.
TL760.W64   629.13   78-15822
ISBN 0-07-071561-0

Book design, Richard A. Wolters.

WHY THIS BOOK

This is the eleventh book I've produced, but in excitement it rates number one! *Silent Flight* has been a lifelong love for me, starting when I was a boy and Great Uncle Sidney made kites for us kids to fly on the Fourth of July. Some of the kites were four feet tall, bigger than I was, and they had tails as long as a house. Great Uncle was my hero; his kites made the Fourth as good as Christmas.

On another July 4 I flew across the Swiss Alps in a gas balloon. That had all the thrills and chills anybody would need but it was only one of the adventures for this book. The biggest challenge of all the silent sports was soaring. My three-hundred-pound fiberglass sailplane, which I flew in the U.S. National competition, took me to twenty-five thousand feet. But for sheer pizzazz the glider flight around the Matterhorn for this book can't be matched. Floating like a bird in a hang glider and plummeting like a rock before a parachute opens are experiences that are dazzling and sometimes wild.

To capture the pleasures of silent flight I took pictures as I went. It was challenging and frustrating at times, but doing self-portraits was fun. How do you put a camera out in space and photograph your balloon's gondola as you drift into Italy? Or do a loop in a sailplane with a camera ahead of the wing taking two pictures a second as your stomach does a flip-flop? The hang glider pictures taken in Lichtenstein over the Prince's palace were triggered by radio, but when I tried using the same radio rig on a motor-drive Nikon to take the parachuting pictures of a jumper leaving the plane, it wouldn't work—the plane's motor set up interfering radio signals. After many failures I finally licked the problem by firing the camera with infrared light. The Nikon folks thought enough of these remote-control sequences to give the pictures in this book a one-man photo exhibition at Nikon House in New York.

It's not a new idea that man has lived at the bottom of a sea of air from time immemorial, and that his very existence has depended on it. He watched the birds for thousands of years and longed to imitate them. He tried every conceivable kind of contraption, but in spite of his technical advancements over the centuries, it's only been in the last two hundred years that he has flown. Hang gliding, the nearest man has come to being a bird, isn't even ten years old. Seventy years ago, when man got into the air with power, he began a technological miracle that led him to the moon.

Now that we have achieved so much with high-powered technology, there seems to be a return to the joy of non-powered flight. We are going to seek *sport* in the air. For years the cry was higher and faster; now it's low and slow. That's what this book is all about. And the wonderful thing about it is that there are five ways into the air.

Make your choice, *take your training,* and get into the world of silent flight.

Richard A. Wolters / December, 1978

CONTENTS

1 KITES

The kite is one of the few objects still in use that has been passed down from antiquity with little or no change. Understandably, its origins were lost in its flight through time. Who invented things like the doll, the ball or the kite? We may never know for sure, but here is a new theory of the origin of the kite.

Legend indicates it appeared first in China. Certainly the Chinese had the tools to make it: bamboo for frames, cloth, and—after 100 A.D.—paper for covering, silk for string, plus, just as important, written language to document their achievements. The kite became part of their folklore—but that doesn't mean they invented it.

DID THE KITE ORIGINATE IN CHINA?

We know for sure that the kite appeared in China two hundred years before the Christian era. It's told that General Han Hsin flew a kite over a palace his troops had under siege to determine the distance between his troops and the palace walls. This story may be the first recorded account of the kite, but it's far from its origin. Scholars have presented various theories. Dr. Joseph Needham, in his book *Science and Civilization in China*, wonders whether the Chinese coolie hat on the end of a string might not have been the idea that sparked the kite concept. A. Waley, writing on folklore, also suggests that the kite's origin was China. Clive Hart, in his two scholarly books *The Dream of Flight* and *Kites: An Historical Survey*, states, "The place of origin of the kite is fairly certain: China. But," he goes on, "who flew the first kite, and what sort of kite it would have been, are questions to which we can give only tentative answers." A. C. Haddon, in his book *The Study of Man*, suggests that the excitement of hauling in a blown-away sail could very well have been the initial idea for the kite, and he therefore suggests seafaring folks as the originators of the kite. It would seem logical to assume that a culture evolving around the sea and the wind would be the first to discover the kite. Since it is known that the kite was used in Malayan religious observances three thousand

The kite maker and the salesman were highly esteemed members of early Chinese society. It's still true about the kite maker.

years ago, it seems plausible that the southwestern or southeastern Pacific could very well have been the birthplace of the kite. Will Yolen, in his book *Kites and Kite Flying*, believes that "The best available evidence indicates that kites evolved somewhere in the southwest Pacific, around the Malay Peninsula." But Will, who first taught me to fly a kite in my adult years, gives no hint of the evidence.

Wyatt Brummitt, in his book *Kites*, gives another vote to China as the likely birthplace. But he believes that kites date back to the beginnings of human cultures; he cites the three-thousand-year-old Malayan kites and a twenty-five-hundred-year-old Egyptian legend about tethered flight. He supports the idea that the earliest kites were made of semi-tropical leaves, but he presents no evidence that they were. They could as easily have been tropical, though such foliage does not grow in China.

If materials and tools were one of the reasons for placing the origin of the kite in China, the same reasons could be given for the islands of the Pacific. Large leaves or mats woven of leaves supported by sticks would have made fine kites thousands of years ago . . . as they do today. The first strings could have been vines. I am suspicious of the scholars' findings for another reason. They did a fantastic job of scouring the literature and artifacts for any reference to the kite. Hart's books are a joy to read. But is the myth of China, as the mother of the kite, perpetuated because she had the first written language? I suspect that Will Yolen is right in his assumption, and A. C. Haddon strikes closer to the heart of the matter in believing that the kite originated in a culture that was seafaring. What the scholars didn't seem to take into consideration are the anthropological indications. The people of the Pacific used leaves, reeds and vines for everything from utensils, building supplies and clothing to tools. They used them for building boats, outriggers and sails. Woven mats for sails are not very different from kites. These migrating seafarers were the greatest navigators in the ancient world, but they didn't get credit for that either because they didn't have a written language to pass their science down through time.

If you were piecing this puzzle together, would you give credit for the invention of the kite to a people who were basically an agricultural society, like the Chinese, or to a people whose very existence depended on the wind?

Let's look at the facts, and you draw your own conclusion. Oceania is a broad term for the territory occupied by all the Pacific Islanders. The people were divided into four basic groups on some ten thousand islands scattered over seven hundred fifty thousand square miles. There are no prehistoric records or, for that matter, historic records of these people until the sixteenth century, when the Europeans made their first sightings of their islands. The Melanesian culture is twenty thousand years old; the little that archeologists have discovered has shown that the migrations and voyages that led to the populating of every habitable island of Oceania started twenty thousand years ago and lasted until about 1200 A.D.

A fishing kite from Banks Island is made from vegetation, bamboo, reeds and leaves.

DID IT FIRST FLY IN THE ISLANDS?

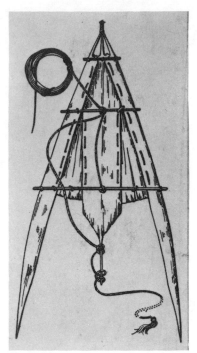

A Solomon Island fishing kite is made from pandanus leaves. The early string was made from vines.

The ancient Pacific peoples' knowledge of navigation can compare with any of the great mental achievements in man's history. The science was lost when the migrations stopped—not only because there was no written record, but because for thousands of years these navigators jealously guarded their secrets. In most primitive cultures the medicine man sat next to the king. In the Oceanian cultures the navigators developed a kind of hereditary priesthood and attained power and rank for themselves second only to the king's. It's believed that by the fourth century A.D. they reached as far as Easter Island. A people with the resourcefulness and creativity to produce the giant idols on lonely Easter Island certainly would have had the ability to create a kite.

It was a pilot, Harold Gatty, a New Zealander who navigated Wiley Post on his famous first flight around the world, who reconstructed the details of the navigation principles of those ancient seafarers. (See *Song of the Sky* by Guy Marchie for a complete account.) These ancient navigators used every element around them as navigating tools—stars, wave motion, tide, currents, sand motion, water temperature, cloud formation, migration of birds, smell, color of the water—but, most important for this discussion, they understood air currents and navigated by them. It was amazing what they could "read" from the wind.

With that as background, we would like to demonstrate, with what little the records reveal, that these master sailors had a more logical reason to originate the kite than the land-oriented Chinese who, the records show, used the kite as a toy, as part of their religious ceremonies and as a tool of war.

THE ISLANDERS' NEED

Of what use would the kite have been to the Oceanian people? This much we know: Anthropologists have found no evidence of toys in their culture. Without a written record to cover their twenty thousand years, we're going to have to do some guesswork to answer the question of whether they originated the kite. There are a few directional arrows.

Progress as we know it was very slow in their society. Education over the long span of time was not handed down from father to son, but from grandfather to grandson. This may have slowed change, but it also time-tested ideas before they were used. That's the way the navigator passed on his skill. The way of life came down through the generations in this tried and proven method. We know that when the Europeans made their first sightings of the Polynesian islands they saw kites go in the air, but on landing they never found them. The kite would have been a natural way of "talking" from island to island. Of course these sightings were in the seventeenth and eighteenth centuries A.D., but couldn't this obvious means of communication be as old as the migrations? It seems strange to take the position that these people, who started their migrations long before the Chinese had the kite, learned about it from the Chinese, who, as far as anthropologists have found, taught them nothing else. We also know from the historical records of the seventeenth century that the kite was used for catching the garfish, a fish that fed on the surface of the water. The islanders' crude fishing lines sank, so the fish could only be taken by using a kite to keep the bait on the surface. That is rather ingenious.

We know, from records kept by the European explorers, that kite fishing and kite signaling were practiced by *all* the islanders. That means that the Indonesians, Micronesians, Melanesians and Polynesians were using the kite. Can we reason that they took this skill with them before the migrations started, instead of assuming that they all learned these techniques independently, three thousand miles apart? If you will accept the proposition that they knew these tricks before the migrations started, it could easily date the kite millennia before the first Chinese records.

Clive Hart, in his book *Kites*, states that there is no firm agreement, but it seems likely that fishing for the garfish by kite was first used in the general area of the Banda Sea and the technique spread both east and west. If this is so, then the myth of China's being the originator of the kite will start to crumble.

Signaling across open sea by kite seems another natural device for the seafarers of Oceania. We know they did it from island to island. What about boat to boat during the time of migration thousands of years ago?

One of the most interesting sights I ever saw took place in the Marshall Islands a few years ago; it may lend credence to my next assumption. I was invited by a team of ornithologists from the Smithsonian Institution to join them on a mission to an unnamed island a day's run from the Bikini Atoll. The island was less than a mile long and about a half-mile wide. Four species of birds roosted on the island at different levels in the trees. It was estimated that the island housed 5 million birds during this nesting season. The startling fact was that each species came from a different place in the Pacific; some traveled thousands of miles to get to this one island. We found no birds on adjacent islands that were only six, eight and ten miles away. Here is

Birds were used as navigation aids for the Island people. It was only natural that birds became part of their kite designs.

Chinese dragon.

what I learned and what the early navigators had to know: The flight path of migrating birds is precise. They start on land and wind up on land. Since the birds cannot rest at sea, the navigators could follow them, knowing they would be led to land.

According to Harold Gatty, that's exactly how the islanders navigated vast stretches of open water. He cites the example of the massive migration of the fifth century A.D., which was rather late in their twenty-thousand-year history of settling the far-flung islands of the Pacific. The Polynesians were crowded on Tahiti, so some of them left to find more land. In their great double sailing canoes they paddled and sailed twenty-five hundred miles to New Zealand, a distance they could have covered in a month going 3.4 miles per hour. Gatty says they followed the long-tailed cuckoo bird on its yearly southwestern migration. Of course a canoe can't keep up with flying birds, but the birds do not go in one mass flight; their migration could take a month. The great boats were spaced out in a long single file. In the daytime, each flock that flew overhead pointed the way; at night, the cry of the cuckoo was their compass.

What is the visibility from canoe to canoe in daylight in the open ocean? It would be half a dozen miles at best. How did they keep track of each other in the vastness of the ocean and get those who strayed off course at night back in line? My assumption is that in the morning they signaled each other with kites. If they knew how to use the kite for signaling from island to island, they certainly could have used it as communication from boat to boat.

QUESTIONING THE CHINA MYTH

Thailand kite.

All the scholars who have tried to piece this puzzle together have documented their findings from the literature and artifacts recovered. The Oceanian people had neither. As far as we know, except for Lapita pottery made by the ancestors of the Polynesians and found only in a small area of the Pacific, they never developed pottery or utensils since they had no need for them. If they wanted a cup or a bowl, a nutshell or seashell sufficed. They were very simple people who lived with what they could carry.

Only thirty years ago I was present during one of the last migrations of the Polynesians when the Bikini Atoll was evacuated. One morning the villagers got their belongings together, and the next morning they were completely settled in their new home, miles away. They lived by making use of natural resources—at this they were very clever. The point is that in their travels, throughout the thousands of years, few if any physical things were introduced to their culture from the outside until the Europeans arrived. The supposition that the Chinese introduced the kite to the Oceanian people does not make anthropological sense. The southwestern people were ingenious and self-sufficient. They had their own need for the kite—and they made it, as they did their early sails, from woven leaves.

I feel safe in assuming that the kite's first use in China was as a toy for the children of an agricultural society. Then, in 200 B.C., according to the first recorded legend, it was put to use as a tool of war. It was said to have been used eight hundred years earlier as part of a religious ceremony in the Malayan Archipelago. The migrations of the Oceanian people had been in progress for millennia before the dating of the kite in Malaya. The sail and the kite are too closely akin to be ignored. If we assume that the seafarers' tools were taken with them and independently discovered thousands of miles apart, then it follows that very early in their history the Oceanian people invented the kite out of need, always the mother of invention.

I propose that the map used by all kite historians showing the origin and distribution of the kite before 1600 A.D. be changed. The theory presented here would give the invention of the kite to the people of Oceania since they had the materials at their fingertips, understood the wind and had a purpose for the invention. It follows, then, that through their travels the kite was introduced to Malaya, then to China.

One last supporting point: If the kite reached Malaya eight hundred years before it was documented in China, and it was part of a religious observance there (which means it must have been much older), why did it take so long for it to appear in the highly developed art and literature of China?

Since it seems likely that garfish were first caught by kite in the Banda Sea, and since this area supports all the other assumptions I've made, I believe that it was in the Banda Sea and the Indonesian area, not in China, that the kite was invented.

The classic design of Japanese kites depicts the confrontation of the priest and the general.

All men have had an atavistic desire to fly; the kite was the first expression of that urge. It's been suggested that man's innate fascination with the heavens stems from his early migrations. Possibly he lightened the drudgery of his travels by fantasies as he watched the birds flying gracefully over obstacles while he toiled. This theory fits the people of Oceania, and it's little wonder that the kite became a strong religious symbol to them. Gods were often represented by birds, and the transition to the kite is easy to understand. Oceanian religious legends told of kite competitions between gods or of the gods struggling with kites against the elements. Actually kites gave these simple people a direct sense of involvement with their deities.

One of the earliest legends was about the wind gods, the two brothers Tane and Rango. The younger, Tane, challenged his brother to a duel with kites. Tane's became entangled in the trees and Rango's kite flew very high. This semi-religious drama has been replayed for generations. It's not clear in the legend what the defeat meant for Tane, but for mortal man, the flier whose kite flew highest was honored by having his kite designated as the god Rango.

Man's eyes and thoughts have always "faced" upward in his religion. Associated with that has been his chanting: He has always sung to his gods. It was no different with kite gods. The flier chanted as he flew his kite and the noisemakers incorporated in the kite's design were considered the god's response.

THE SPIRIT ... THE WARRIOR ... AND JUST FUN

Japanese centipede.

All sizes of kites and all sizes and kinds of people come out each year to the kite festival in Central Park, New York. They fly miniatures of less than an inch to the big ones that take two or three people to walk them into the park. They all have one wish . . . to be up there with their kite.

THE KITE IN OCEANIA

No other people used the kite in so many aspects of their lives. We have tried to show from their practical use of the kite that the people of Oceania used it before the Chinese did. Other societies used it in spiritual or religious ceremonies and also in a social manner, but there seems to be no other record except in Oceania of the judicial use of the kite. It was in their folklore and in their games. It was a means of communication and a good reason to throw a party. They fished with the kite, used it for meteorology, navigated with it and used it to scare their enemies. For an item as simple as a few sticks, rushes, bark, plaited leaves and fiber string, it was a most important and essential part of the islanders' life and thought.

THE KITE TRAVELS THROUGHOUT THE ORIENT

By the fifth or sixth century A.D. the literature of Korea contained stories that seem very similar to the early kite stories of China. War seems again to have been the basic use for the kite. An early Korean legend tells of kites carrying fire over the enemy walls or, in a somewhat more fanciful version, carrying men into the enemy stronghold.

It's thought that when the kite reached Japan it immediately became part of religious ceremonies. Early Japanese legends also refer often to man-carrying kites. There were stories of bandits invading palaces and robbers stealing the fish made of gold that adorned the temple in Nagoya. Ishikawa Goyamen and his gang, who used kites to reach the gold, were caught and boiled in oil. The Japanese were infatuated with the idea of man-carrying kites and on several occasions laws forbidding the construction of extra-large kites were issued by the nobility, who were afraid of an invasion from the sky.

Korean fighter.

It's interesting to note that in Korea, Japan, Thailand, Cambodia, Indonesia, India and practically all the rest of the Orient, kite flying became the national sport. Each country came up with hundreds of individual designs for their ceremonial and "just fun" kites. The kite maker was an artisan whose produce was not a toy but a sophisticated precision instrument that played an important role in almost every facet of Eastern thought. The kite was the favorite theme of the poet; the romantic used his skill to drop message-bearing kites into the hands of his loved one who, according to tradition, was kept in strict seclusion; the priests sent kites into the heavens as offerings to the deities; the fortune-teller read into the kite's flight the flier's future.

FIGHTING KITES

We Westerners don't think of kite flying as being competitive, but it is.

Competition kites, the fighter kites, of all the Oriental nations are very similar in design. Many consider the Japanese variation of the fighter, called the Nagasaki, as the best. To the Indian or the Korean that's a challenge.

Kites were an outlet for man's competitive spirit. For many hundreds of years kite fighting was the national sport in the Orient. Public contests between towns were festive occasions: wagers were made and crowds cheered for their heroes. Or it might be an "amateur" event. Any individual putting up his kite knew it wouldn't take long for another kite to be in the sky to meet his challenge. It might take place in a park, an open field or from a flat rooftop.

New Year's in Japan is the traditional kite flying day. These festivities are taking place in front of Edo Castle. Mount Fuji is in the background.

The fighter kites are in a class by themselves. Putting any kite up is fun, but the fighters add another dimension to the sport; they are extremely maneuverable. Fighters are so light and delicately balanced that it takes only the slightest breeze to get them airborne. It takes no running. All the flier needs is an assistant to hold the kite about fifty or more feet away and let it go when the line is taut. A few deft pulls on the string will have it zooming upward to meet the breeze.

The Indian fighter is a most extraordinary kite. It can be made to dive at about thirty miles an hour, stop and pinwheel at any altitude. It can dive at the ground and at knee height be reversed to climb back up, or it can be pinwheeled at head height, turned within its own length and darted back overhead. It's understandable why some kite fliers won't even bother flying anything but an Indian fighter.

Indian Fighter kite.

Kite flying became such a serious problem for the farmers of China that it was finally declared illegal to fly them. The hordes of people running over the open fields ruined the crops.

Once the flier learns how to maneuver the kite in all directions he is then ready to do battle. He prepares the first two hundred feet of the string nearest the kite by dipping it into a compound containing powdered glass and egg white. By custom, the glassed string was colored and attached to a white flying string. The game is to cut the other fellow's string. There are many techniques and tricks, but the basic idea is to feel the touch of the two strings when they meet—and then start the attacking maneuver. When the strings meet you should let out your string very slowly. If your string stops it will be cut by the opponent's glass. If your string is below, you should make your kite climb, thus hanging the opponent's kite on your string and cutting it. If your kite comes down to meet the other kite, then you should let string out faster and start your kite in a new direction. Rolling your kite will keep the pressure on his string and moving the kite out will make your string act as a saw.

Some fighters have devised ways of capturing the cut string and bringing down the opponent's kite as a trophy. The winner must be careful when retrieving his own kite that the free string doesn't cut his line.

This game has been played for hundreds of years in the Orient. Today you can see kite fighting in New York City's Central Park if the wind is right.

KITES ON THE WESTERN SCENE

Some believe that the kite spread across Asia to the Mediterranean, but there is no clear-cut evidence of this. It never took hold there as a religious symbol, sporting game or child's toy, as it was used in China. There is no real evidence that other ancient cultures even knew about the kite. Isolated stories emerged from Egypt, Crete and Greece, but fact and fantasy are mixed in the legends. Could Icarus have been flying a man-carrying kite?

As early as 1326 an unfinished sketch by Walter de Milemete shows a pennon kite being used to drop a fire bomb over a besieged city. Then three hundred years passed with only an occasional mention of kites of any kind in the literature. It's not until 1618 that the kite makes its appearance in the West as a toy for children. It's surmised that the Dutch sailors brought the kite to Europe from the Orient. By the late seventeenth century the kite was commonplace from England to Italy. The word "kite" wasn't applied to the man-made object until the sixteenth century; it's named after a kind of hawk known for its ability to hover in the air.

THE EIGHTEENTH-CENTURY KITE

Isaac Newton as a boy was playing with kites as the seventeenth century ended. Brewster, his biographer, said that he introduced the flying of paper kites and changed their design to make them fly better. He also attached lanterns of crumpled paper with candles to the tail to frighten the country folks into thinking them comets. During the eighteenth century the kite was not only a popular toy with the children of Europe, but more important it was used in scientific experiments that continued up to the twentieth century . . . until the invention of the

This is the earliest known illustration of a European kite. It was drawn by Walter de Milemete and shows in the left-hand portion a kite flying over a fortification and dropping a fire bomb. The soldiers on the right are using a winch to fly the kite.

airplane. It all started in 1749 with Alexander Wilson and Thomas Melvill, who were exploring the temperature of the upper atmosphere by sending thermometers up on trains of kites. The most celebrated research with the kite was Ben Franklin's electrical experiment in 1752. Those experiments were so hazardous that scientists today wonder why Franklin didn't kill himself.

After his electrical experiments Franklin went on to "play" with the kite. He rigged a big one and towed himself across a pond in the summer and did the same thing again on ice skates in the winter. It is surprising that men like Joseph Priestley, who wrote much about Franklin's experiments, and Franklin himself never seemed to take a hard look at the kite itself and try to understand the principle of lift. It's fun to speculate what might have happened if the Western world had taken to the kite as the Orient did. Would the great minds of the Renaissance have discovered lift if they had paid more attention to the kite and the soaring birds? The principle of the glider was probably at the fingertips of the Greek Archytas as early as 400 B.C. By the time of Leonardo most forms of flight had either been proposed or tried: kites, gliders, balloons, helicopters, parachutes. If the kite had been an every-day item, as it was in the Orient, would it have pointed men like Leonardo in the right direction?

Kites continued to be used through the eighteenth century as a vehicle for experimenting in the atmosphere, though little attention was paid to their design. The Western kite was an inefficient, crude flying machine in contrast to what had been designed in the Orient centuries earlier.

George Pocock, an English schoolmaster, made history in 1825 by attaching a "team" of eight-foot kites to a carriage. He managed to skitter at twenty-five miles per hour across more than one hundred miles of English countryside, avoiding trees, church steeples and such. He gets the title of the first successful invention with the kite. Sailors picked up

THE NINETEENTH-CENTURY WORKHORSE OF THE SKY

Pocock's idea and used high-flying kites to tow their boats home from the fishing grounds. Pocock also demonstrated how a kite could be used to rescue shipwrecked seamen. He hoisted his own son in a kite-borne chair from a beach to the top of a two-hundred-foot seaside cliff.

It is said that during the Civil War the Yankees took a leaf from an old Chinese book and used the kite to drop bundles of leaflets offering amnesty to Confederates who would lay down their arms. During the Boer War, six-unit trains of hexagonal kites were used to carry spotters over the enemy lines.

By this time man was clamoring to get into the air. The kite held the secret of heavier-than-air flight and had been around for three thousand years—but no one saw it.

THE THEORY OF LIFT WAS THERE ALL THE TIME

From ancient times man has dreamed about flying; the irony is that he had the key to the theory of flight all the time. A child's kite is just as much an airfoil as a jet wing . . . both produce lift. Any object that deflects the flow of air to create lift and thus rise on air is called an airfoil. It foils the air into producing a work load—lift. And lift is the overcoming of gravity.

Isaac Newton, who flew kites as a boy, gave the world the theory of lift in his "Third Law of Motion," which states, "For every action there is an equal and opposite reaction." The simplest way to understand the theory of lift is to comprehend how a kite flies, be it a leaf kite on the end of a vine flown by a Micronesian boy thousands of years ago, the highly sophisticated Indian fighter kite, or Ben Franklin's crude, pear-shaped kite rigged for his electrical experiments.

Newton's Third Law of Motion is easy to understand. The favorite science class demonstration is to have two students on roller skates stand facing each other, toe to toe. One of them is asked to push the other away. On doing so the one pushed goes backward, but so does the one who did the pushing . . . action and reaction go together.

Substitute the wind and the kite for the two boys. The wind pushes the kite and produces lift and the kite pushes the wind, which is deflected downward. It's that simple and it applies as well to the sailplane, the airplane or the jet. There is no difference in the theory, whether it's the plane that is thrust through the air to make a "wind" or the kite standing still on its tether with the wind rushing past it. Lift is produced by the interaction of the forces.

In the United States, for the past thirty or forty years we've been taught that the theory of flight was developed from Bernoulli's principle, a hydrodynamic law that led to the postulation that lift results from a difference of pressure above and below the wing. This theory, which is not taught in Europe, is in disrepute because it leaves us helpless to explain such things as how a plane can fly upside down or how a jet can fly with a symmetrical airfoil (one that has the same curve top and bottom).

Lift is produced by the airfoil's pushing the air down. The object held at an inclined angle meets the air at an "angle of attack." The kite, held facing the wind by its bridle, is a perfect and simple explanation of

It's thought that the Dutch first brought the kite to Europe. It was considered a child's toy. The eighteenth-century German artist Chodowiecki shows children at play.

lift. By moving the bridle, changing the angle at which the kite attacks the oncoming wind, we can make the kite fly high or low.

Isaac Newton gave us the theory of lift, but it wasn't until Sir George Cayley designed his first glider kite in 1804 that we saw the theory put into practice. His kite could be called the first modern configuration of the airplane. It had a fixed main wing and an adjustable rear rudder and elevator. Although Cayley was working toward a glider, he used the kite form for his experimentation. By bowing the kite he anticipated the William Eddy kite, which came along at the end of the century.

The Eddy kite, invented in the early 1890s, was truly the first genuine advance in *Western* kite design (though the Japanese had known about it for centuries) since the development of the diamond-shaped kite in the Renaissance. The Eddy kite introduced the important principle of the dihedral to give stability to a flying object. The Eddy kite was so stable it needed no tail. The bowed kite presented to the wind a more streamlined angle. When a gust of wind lifted one side of the angled surface, the other side was forced down. The downward pressure on that side had the same effect as if more wind were blowing against it. The result was lift. The downed side of the kite raised itself, equalizing the pressure on both faces of the kite. Manned flight was not possible until this principle of flight stability had been discovered.

The last decade of the nineteenth century saw a lot of inventors seeking to put all the principles that the kite had finally taught man into a package that would allow manned flight. The next step in that development was the invention of the cellular or box kite by Lawrence Hargrave. While Eddy was a newspaperman and kites were his fun in life, Hargrave was a serious inventor seeking the answer to manned flight problems.

THE SEARCH FOR FLIGHT STARTS IN EARNEST

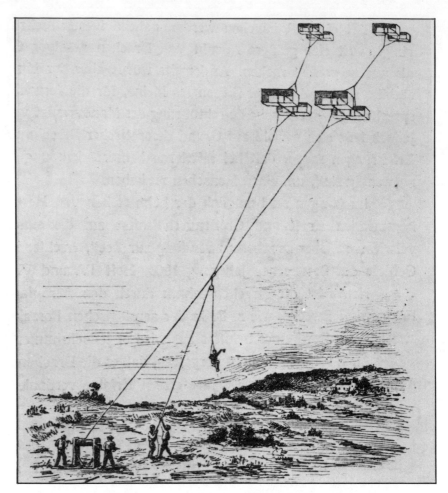

There were those who were convinced that the way to free flight was by putting a man up in a kite and once he was stable to start a motor-driven propeller and cut him loose from the ground. Captain B. F. S. Baden-Powell patented a levitor kite which could lift a man a hundred feet into the air. It was used during the Boer War for putting military spotters in the air.

Many serious-minded inventors took the Hargrave kite as the fundamental ingredient for powered flight. The boxes or cells could be added together in the manner of children's building blocks with an infinite number of possibilities. Alexander Graham Bell came up with hundreds of designs, using over three thousand cells in one kite, hoping such a design would be successful for manned flight. Actually, the thinking seemed very logical. If a kite that was strong, light and stable could be built, all it needed was motor power and the result would be manned flight.

The Wright brothers proved that the error with Hargrave's and Bell's theories was in their seeking inherent stability. Hargrave's first plan called for a train of man-lifting kites to be raised and anchored to the ground with a motor attached to the lowest kite. Once the pilot was carried aloft and the whole contraption was facing upwind, the motor would be started, the anchor hauled up and the trip begun. Later his plan called for a motor connected to the series of box kites, but with no plan for maneuvering in flight. The Wright brothers consciously chose unstable flying surfaces that had to be controlled by the pilot. The first Kitty Hawk "kite" was a biplane, but, unlike the Hargrave box design, it had no vertical stabilizers. They flew it with a system of lines that controlled the unstable lifting surfaces. They learned to warp the wings for flight stability by flying their first glider as a kite. It took the world a long time to make the transition from kite to manned flight.

Once the airplane was invented the kite was given back to the kids, and there it stayed for a long time. It was perfectly all right for grown men in the Western world to strike a ball with a club and chase it all over the countryside trying to put it into a hole in the ground, but if such a man flew a kite he was considered odd. It has been only recently that "doing your own thing" has become accepted in our society. No longer is it necessary for a grown man who wants to fly a kite to have to cajole or bribe a kid to stand by his side to make it all seem legitimate.

Seventy-five million kites were sold in the United States this year and that's not just a lot of wind. Kites are going back in the air all over the country. You can pay anything from fifty cents for a two-sticker to a thousand dollars for a hand-painted dragon kite from Japan.

It had been close to half a century since I'd put toys aside and set my mind to the work of the real world when Will Yolan, the king of fliers, suggested I accompany him to a kite festival and contest. Being a soaring pilot, almost anything to do with air interested me. I must say that kites were the lesser side of it. It was fun, though, and I enjoyed watching Will teaching all shapes and sizes of people to prance around the field pulling on strings. The airfoil of one buxom woman had more lift than her kite, but that was only noticed in the third event. The last contest of the day was called the Open. As judge, Will was in his glory. A few seconds before the whistle (the signal to man or woman your kites) Will handed me one and said, "Fly it!" On the "go" signal I let the kite slip into the wind. To my surprise . . . while I stood still, up it went. The buxom one, looking over her shoulder as she pranced around, still without any lift to her kite, smashed me to the ground. Screaming "I've been fouled!" I hung onto my string as if it were my last support. I went on to get my kite up first and highest and win the

GO FLY A KITE . . . HAVE FUN

HOW DO YOU FLY 'EM?

Will Yolan, the recognized king of the kite fliers, teaches a class how to fly 'em. He originated the use of the fishing rod launch. He has been advocating a kite contest in the Olympics and starts the kids out at a young age. At right a contest is about to begin. On the next page Yolan teaches the author how to put up a sled kite.

major event of the day. Actually, I won first and second prize. That other contestant with the big airfoil got her string caught in mine. I made a deal with her on the spot . . . or ground. If she let her string go, her kite would go up with mine. She won second place. At the presentation ceremony Will disqualified us both for "unsportsman and woman behavior." News travels fast; my wife wasn't about to believe my story when I came home with two new store-bought kites.

As starters, that's pretty good for any sport, but the point is this: Of all the flying sports this is the one that requires little or no training. You need an open area, wind at your back (so it feels the same on both ears) and some common sense.

Don't fly kites over power lines. You could kill yourself, black out a whole community or start a disastrous fire. Use the eyes in back of your head so you can see where you are running. Don't fly near roadways. Diving kites have frightened motorists and caused accidents. Don't try to be a Ben Franklin and fly kites in a storm or you might become a lightning rod. Don't fly near airports or in low visibility. Don't use metal frames, metal tails or metallic Mylar in the construction of a kite. Don't hang fireworks or sparklers on a kite. With a big kite, in a heavy wind, it makes sense to wear gloves; nylon lines can cut hands.

The best time to fly a kite is after a storm has passed when unstable clearing winds move in. Here's some wind information:

1 to 3 mph . . . Smoke drifts up lazily . . . flags don't do much . . . kites won't do much either.
4 to 7 mph . . . Leaves rustle . . . flags show their colors . . . fly the kite. Light ones and the non-ridged will do best.
8 to 12 mph . . . Leaves dance . . . flags and girls' skirts wave . . . try even the box kite.
13 to 18 mph . . . Papers fly down the street . . . trees dance . . . anything will fly, and if you have a heavy kite, wear gloves.
19 to 24 mph . . . Trees sway . . . hats fly . . . strings break, but go on and try it.
25 mph and up . . . Stay home and read or take a kite whose loss won't make you cry.

Launching the kite is easy in a good wind. It's the light wind that causes the problems. Fighter kites, the flat dragons and the non-ridged kites are the easiest to get up in light air. The bigger stick kites may require some assistance. You must get a kite up on the first pull when there is little wind. Walk the kite downwind a hundred paces and either have it stand itself (square bottoms and box kites will do this) or have someone stand behind the kite and hold it. Wait for a breeze and yell to your assistant to let go. Pull the string in hand-over-hand in quick yanks, walking backward as you do it. Drop the string on the ground as you go so it won't get tangled. Wind near the ground is usually crazy; with luck you'll get the kite up into the firmer flow. Your hand will tell you when the kite is ready for more string. Slight pressure means more string. If it drops, a yank will get it climbing. Alternate string out and yanks. If it catches a strong breeze up there, don't let it climb to too sharp an angle overhead. If it flies too far forward it'll nose under and dive. Near the ground that's boomsville.

The flying bridle and the point where it attaches to the line are most important to flight control. This connecting point determines the flight attitude—the angle at which the kite will meet the wind. This determines the angle of attack, which in a kite is the same as the angle of incidence. In an airplane the angle of incidence is the angle at which the wing is attached to the fuselage of the plane. The designer of the craft sets that angle. The pilot then flies the plane so the wing meets the air at an angle of attack that will make the airflow produce lift. These two angles become the same thing in kites. In a light wind a steeper angle is needed, so make the hitch at a lower point on the bridle. In a strong wind move the hitch up. Too low a bridle connection can send the kite into a series of lateral loops; too high a connection will reduce the efficiency and make it flop like wash on a line.

The connection is made easy by using a spin fisherman's swivel snap fastener tied to the flying line. This eliminates knotting the line to the bridle and makes for a fast connection. Don't assume that the bridle point of attachment is correct on store-bought kites. Except for the non-ridged parawing and parafoil kites, you should always experiment with the bridle point of attachment.

Landing a kite presents a problem only in strong winds. If it gets too far forward it may loop or dive. A good trick in a strong wind is to have one person reel the kite in while an assistant walks the kite down. The assistant uses a glove and lets the string go under his arm as he walks forward. When the kite gets too far overhead and starts to dive, the walker releases the line. The kite loses lift and flutters down and backward on the wind. When the line becomes taut the kite flies again, but at a lower angle. This is repeated until it comes to hand.

The kite-line reel is an important part of the equipment. Winding in a thousand feet of line can be tedious, monotonous work. The reel can be anything from a stick or a beer can to an expensive deep-sea-fishing reel. The important thing is that its core be big so you gather in a good amount of line with each revolution. I made one out of the front hub of a bicycle wheel. It's crude, but it'll hold a mile of line and the ball bearings make it run as free as the wind. All sorts of reels can be bought or improvised; it's a matter of one that fits your fancy and pocketbook.

Flying a kite with rod and reel is a fine system. A short deep-sea rod is best and the reel should have a geared drive. The rod becomes an extension of your arm. The kite can be launched very conveniently with the rod. The kite is whirled overhead; back and forth it goes in its own wind. Slowly the line is let out until the kite is cast up into the breeze . . . up it goes. This saves all the running business, which good kite fliers leave to the kids. It also gives the pilot more control; his whole body and the extension of his arm can be used to make a six-foot yank on the string . . . even a gorilla couldn't do that.

LINE CLIMBERS ... DROPPERS ... AND THINGS

Sending messages up to a kite is almost as old as kite flying. The simplest is a square piece of paper with a hole in the center. Slit the paper, put the center hole on the line, then tape the slot closed. If you curl the corners of the paper it'll pinwheel as it goes up. The same thing can be done with a straw. Slit the straw lengthwise, put it on the string and tape the slit closed. Attach a paper sail to the straw and up it'll ride.

Dropping parachutes or paper gliders is another project which is fun. The "thing" is attached to the flying line and a releasing mechanism is used. A simple releaser can be made from a piece of punk. Connect the punk in the middle of the line that holds the object to be dropped. Light the punk and let out the flying line. In five or ten minutes the punk will burn through the holding line and the object will drop.

You can get as elaborate with climbers and droppers as you want. Radio-controlled hooks, which open electronically, send up a bag of flour and then "bomb" it.

Putting up trains of kites can be lots of fun too. The trick is to use a strong-flying, reliable performer for the anchor kite. Put the first kite up about a hundred yards. Fly the second kite. When it's up about fifty yards, cut the line and attach it to the main line. Let out another fifty yards of the main line. Keep repeating this until you run out of kites or string. The trick is to use high fliers for the additional kites. You want them to fly above the main line. Records of over a hundred kites on one line have been claimed, and I know they are true because kite people don't lie. But you'll have lots of sport putting up two or three or maybe, if you're rich and lucky, a dozen.

YOU SHOULD KNOW ... IF YOU ARE GOING TO FLY A KITE

Of all the sports in the air, kite flying is the least organized. You can be an enthusiastic member of the kite-flying fraternity for a buck or two, the cost of string and a kite. Or you can spend hundreds of dollars on the same items plus a reel. There are, too, organizations such as the International Kitefliers Association, whose motto is "Worldwide Friendship through Kite Flying." Free membership can be had by writing to the Association at 321 East 48th Street, New York, New York 10017. The organization, which sponsors kite contests from time to time, has done much to get city kids out into the parks for a day's fun. A more organized group is the American Kitefliers Association, P.O. Box 1511, Silver City, New Mexico 88061. They publish a quarterly magazine called *Kite Tales*. It covers everything—designs, building, recreational flying, competition and the scientific study of aerodynamics. The annual dues are $10.

All flying sports are regulated by the government *except* kiting, both the kind on a string and the kite's big sister, the hang glider.

Practically every state has kite festivals and contests. The list of cities, large and small, would almost be endless. The simplest way to find out about such events is to check with the local parks, recreation department, Chamber of Commerce, police department and stores that

1.

2.

3.

4.

5.

There are as many kinds of kites as people at a festival. Picture 1 is a home-made copy of a Marcini rigged jib kite. Picture 2 is Betty Bruhaus's Delta kite. She designed it and she's flying it. Picture 3 is an Air Scoop manufactured by Synestructics. Picture 4 is a home-made job based on a design by Hargrave. Picture 5 is a hand-painted Hexagon Three Stick, an Indian design.

sell kites (check the Yellow Pages). They'll know about forthcoming events, as will the local newspaper and library.

Kites can be bought at most novelty, toy or candy stores. Retailing of kites in the last ten years has grown by 400 percent. Gayla and Hi-Flier have become the two big manufacturers, but if you want something beyond the candy-store variety you will have to go to one of the specialists, such as Airplane Kite Co. of Roswell, New Mexico 88201; or Nantucket Kiteman, Nantucket, Massachusetts 02554. For tetrahedral kites write Geodestix, P.O. Box 308, Spokane, Washington 99211. Of course, the best sources of all for the one hundred or so small companies in the kite and supplies business are the stores that deal exclusively in kites. They not only do a big business at their store locations, but they do catalogue business by mail. These stores are a grown-up child's delight. Here are the best-known ones: Go Fly A Kite, 1613 Second Avenue, New York, New York 10028; Come Fly A Kite, 900 North Pt., Ghiradelli Sq., San Francisco, California 94109; and A. D. Goddard, P.O. Box 133, Otsego, Michigan 49078, which is a storehouse of information about kites, kite manufacturers and where to buy special equipment. The Kite Factory, P.O. Box 9081, Seattle, Washington 98109, packages great kites and sets up kite tours to the Orient and other glamorous places.

For a complete listing of manufacturers, contests around the world or a general source on kiting, read Will Yolen's book, *The Complete Book of Kites and Kite Flying*, published by Simon and Schuster. The book is informative and makes interesting reading because Will has flown kites all over the world and with tongue in cheek is proclaimed the World Champion Kite Flyer. For many, the sport of kiting is in the making of the kite. There is no better book for the maker than *Kite Craft* by L. S. and J. H. Newman, published by Crown. This book covers the history, aerodynamics, construction techniques and decorating of all kinds of kites. The most scholarly and one of the most interesting books on this sport is Clive Hart's *Kites*: *An Historical Survey*, published by Praeger. This book traces the kite in folklore, art, religion and early literature. An inexpensive book to get young people interested in kites is the Golden Press Handbook called *Kites*, by Wyatt Brummitt. It covers all phases of the sport in an easy-to-read, concise manner. The well-equipped kite flier should have, besides different kinds of kites for different weather conditions, a wind meter to establish wind speed and a range finder. The Dwyer Wind Meter, made by Dwyer Manufacturing Co., Michigan City, Indiana, is a good one. It can be purchased through the Edmund Scientific Company, Barrington, New Jersey 08007. This catalogue has a lot of good items for anyone building his own kites. A good range finder for the kiter is made by Ranging, Inc., P.O. Box 9106, Rochester, New York. With the distance and the angle of the kite line known, it's easy to figure the height of the kite. "How high is it?" is the question bystanders and kiters alike ask, half wishing they were up there with it.

Go Fly A Kite Store in New York.

2
BALLOONING

At fifty-four minutes past one o'clock on November 21, 1783, Major Pilatre de Rozier and the Marquis d' Arlandes ascended safely over some tall trees and up majestically into the atmosphere. All of Paris turned out for the event; four hundred thousand saw the happening and it's been said that it was the largest crowd that had ever assembled. And so ended or began man's long quest for flight, as the two successfully made their thrity-minute balloon passage over Paris. It was reported from below that the marquis stood on one side of the wicker basket mechanically waving his hat while the major stood on the other side at rigid salute. Between them stood the "cloud" maker, a pot of burning chopped wool and straw producing quantities of noxious smoke. What their thoughts were aloft was not recorded.

At ten minutes before seven o'clock, almost two hundred years later, over the lush countryside of New Jersey, another ascent was made in a hot-air balloon. It wasn't a marquis or a major in the gondola; it was I. Theirs was the first and mine could have been the millionth ascent, but our reactions couldn't have been very different. Only one word repeatedly seemed to pass my lips—"Wow!" The first ascent in a balloon is a fantasy come true. The moment before takeoff I was standing under my own power, out in the open countryside. The moment after takeoff, with no physical effort on my part, my perspective on the world around me changed dramatically, To be snatched away effortlessly from all that is familiar is an experience that should not be missed. The marquis and the major couldn't have been more elated two centuries earlier; we were all doing the same thing.

Another thing we had in common was that none of us knew much about balloon flight. I just believed in the contraption and wanted the experience. History says that not only didn't those first aeronauts know what made a balloon fly, but the *inventors* of the hot-air balloon, Joseph and Étienne Montgolfier, didn't know either. In spite of being well educated in the sciences of the day, Joseph discovered the hot-air balloon using erroneous Artistotelian logic. "If clouds can float in the sky," he reasoned, "why not capture the cloud and enclose it in a bag?" The cloud would seek its place in the order of things, according to Aristotle, and Joseph reasoned that the bag would be lifted by the cloud and carry objects with it. He proceeded to build a cloud by burning anything that would produce black noxious smoke—wool, straw, rotten meat and old shoes.

Scanning through history, we find it amazing that the balloon took so long to be invented. In the third century B.C., the Greek mathematician Archimedes set down the principle that makes balloons work. He states that when a gas of lesser density than air is enclosed in a container, the difference between the gas and the air it displaces causes the container to rise. In the Middle Ages the scholar Albertus Magnus reported that when one blows warm air from the lungs into a bladder it is measurably lighter than when empty. There it was . . . but strangely, this first flight, made under the direction of the King of France, by order of the Academy of Science of Paris, in a time when science was a flourishing fad, was a success while the principle of the flight was not known or understood. Even the esteemed Dr. Franklin, who was in the crowd, saw the merit of the invention but not the principle. When someone standing next to him skeptically asked, "What good is it?" Franklin is said to have replied, "What good is a newborn baby?" He immediately wrote back to the United States describing the contraption and expounding on its potential military merits.

No breakthrough in knowledge was needed to bring about the invention of the hot-air balloon, so it is strange that it took so long in coming. Once it arrived, small versions became children's toys. A globe-shaped paper bag with a candle suspended below made an ideal plaything for the children of Europe. The question arises, how does it happen the Chinese didn't stumble on this invention centuries earlier? They made paper lanterns and put candles in them. If they had closed the top of the lantern they would have had the hot-air balloon.

The paper envelope was the key to the invention of the hot-air balloon. Ironically, sixteen hundred years after the Chinese invented paper, the Montgolfier brothers, whose family business was papermaking, invented the contraption. The Montgolfier experiments started a year before the first successful manned flight. They began indoors where the first ascents were made by heating envelopes of hot air and sending them to the ceiling. The first outdoor try carried the heated bag seventy feet before it lost its buoyancy. By June 1783 they assembled a bag so big it took eight men to hold it on the ground. On release it went to six thousand feet. That news traveled to Paris and caused much ex-

All of Paris turned out for the event. Just 200 years ago, it was man's first successful flight.

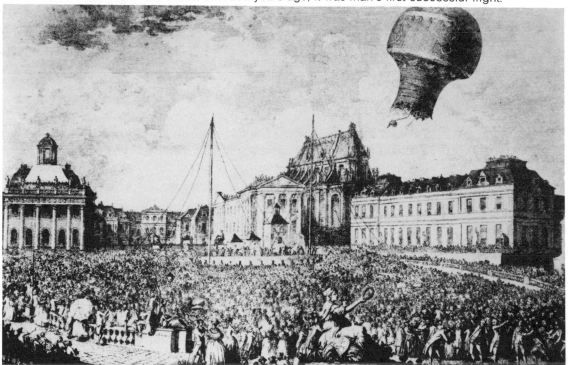

Ten days after the Montgolfier hot-air flight, J. A. C. Charles and his brother made the first gas flight.

citement in the Academy of Science. The brothers were invited to the capital to demonstrate their aerostat. They immediately went to work preparing more balloons, but in the meantime the Academy authorized a young scientist, J. A. C. Charles, to investigate this matter. Using hydrogen, the discovery of Henry Cavendish, he theorized that an envelope would rise if it entrapped enough of a lighter-than-air gas. Ten days after the first Montgolfier flight, Charles and his brother made a two-hour, twenty-seven-mile flight. The balloon age had arrived.

THE THEORY

Archimedes had it right. The theory of lift as applied to a balloon is the same for both the gas and the hot-air versions. In one the lift comes from the gas, and in the other it's produced by air that is heated and thereby made lighter than the ambient air.

We'll confine most of our discussion to the hot-air balloon. It has virtually replaced the gas balloon because hydrogen, the most abundant and best lifting gas, is highly explosive, and helium is so expensive that one flight would cost thousands of dollars.

The theory of flight of both balloons is rather simple. The gas balloon is not filled to full capacity for takeoff. As it ascends, the outside air pressure on the bag becomes less and less. The gas in the bag expands. Since the gas is lighter than air the exit or overflow port is at the bottom of the bag. But it cannot relieve the pressure fast enough, so the bag could rupture. The bag is thus only partially filled so there is

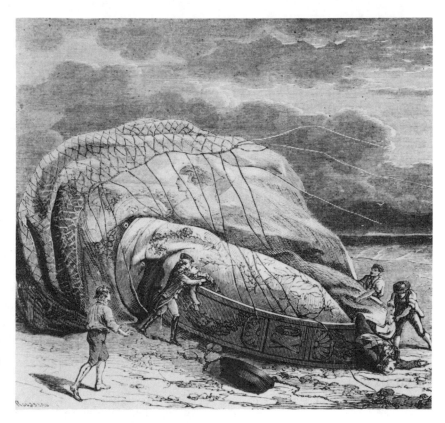

The first balloon tragedy occurred when Pilatre de Rozier tried to cross the English Channel. De Rozier was the pilot of the first flight over Paris in 1783 and in 1785 the first air fatality.

The world's first hydrogen balloon landed in a small village in France and scared the village people into attack. They tied the balloon to a donkey's tail and sent him down the road. Below, Napoleon's army try using the balloon for spotting.

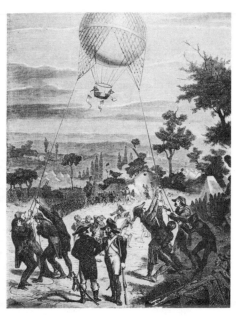

room left for expansion. An inflated gas balloon is controlled by venting the gas to lose lift, or by releasing sand or ballast to gain altitude. The size of the bag will determine the payload it can carry plus the all-important ballast. A gas balloon will rise and reach an equilibrium height. Many factors influence that equilibrium. Cooling will cause the gas to contract; an increase in solar heat will make it expand. A cooling balloon will descend, and to make it go back up sand must be thrown out. The opposite is true when the balloon is warmed. To make it descend, gas must be vented to bring it back to equilibrium. Flying a gas balloon is balancing the gas against the ballast—and the flight is over when too much gas has been vented or when the sand is running low.

The hot-air balloon is the practical answer to the sport. Fifteen dollars' worth of propane gas to heat the air will accomplish what twenty-five hundred dollars' worth of helium or eight hundred dollars' worth of hydrogen will do. Hot-air balloons are more maneuverable than gas balloons because rapid changes in lift can be made without affecting the duration of the flight. The lifting force is a result of the temperature and/or the density differential between the air inside the envelope and the air outside. The amount of heating depends on the conditions of the outside air. Dry cool air is more dense than moist warm air. Dry cool air requires less heating of the envelope to make the density differential for lift. Lift is lost the higher the hot-air balloon goes because the density differential between the two air masses becomes less as the air outside becomes rarer. The propane burners become less efficient with altitude. All this is not difficult to deal with; it means that under adverse conditions a flight may have to be cut short by about 30 percent because of low fuel.

Every balloon flight is an adventure—that is the attraction. Once the balloon is launched, its direction and speed depend entirely on the wind. It all depends on the air mass the pilot finds. Of course it's not completely blind flying. Every weather forecast gives the general pattern and movement of the air mass for that locality; direction and speed of the winds aloft can be obtained from aviation weather stations. But no matter how you cut that cookie, all the balloonist can say after getting his information is "Up to six thousand feet I think I'll be going

There are three basic instruments. On the left is a variometer. It indicates instantly up and down movement. In the middle is a pyrometer, which gives a direct readout of the temperature inside the envelope. On the right is an altimeter, which reads out changes in air pressure and provides a reading of altitude in feet.

The Rip Panel or the Deflation Port empties the balloon of hot air on landing so that the occupants won't be dragged across the ground. On normal landings the rip line is pulled on contact with the ground. In high-wind landings it'll be pulled, providing the rate of descent is minimal, while the balloon is several feet off the ground.

northeast at about six miles per hour. Above that I'll be headed north at eight." It's not exactly pinpointing a destination as you can do in most other forms of flight. A good balloon pilot never waits until he has to land because of low fuel. He'll leave plenty of margin for safety. The pilot has vertical control, but practically none horizontally. Unless adverse winds develop, landing is as controlled as the takeoff. A balloon in the sky is a beautiful sight, but it's an awkward elephant to fly.

THE BALLOON CONSTRUCTION

Two modern-day developments are responsible for the sudden rebirth of this two-hundred-year-old sport: the propane burners that can give out 1 million BTUs of heat, and ripstop nylon. This fabric is light and impregnated to make it tough. The cloth, cut in gores, is sewn together with a few miles of nylon thread. The number of gores depends on the size and manufacturer's design. Load tapes are sewn in up the center of the gores. A self-closing maneuvering vent is cut in the side of the envelope and the rip panel is at the top; both openings are activated by ropes that come down the inside of the balloon to the basket.

The weight of the gondola, crew, propane, etc., is supported by the envelope through the load tapes. Some manufacturers run horizontal tapes for extra support; these are sometimes incorporated into the edge of the gore. At the opening at the bottom of the balloon, the envelope is attached to the load ring or burner platform by stainless-steel cables. The gondola is also attached to the load ring by steel cable. Incidentally, it's called a gondola if it's made of aluminum or fiberglass; if it's wicker, it's a basket.

Two propane tanks are carried securely in the gondola. There are two supply lines to the burner. One goes through the regulator and is controlled by a valve. The regulator adjusts the pressure of gas supplied to the burner. The other line bypasses the regulator and feeds the burner directly from the tank. This line is controlled by the blast or tooter valve. It's used when a lot of heat is needed in a hurry.

There are two kinds of envelopes. Both have the vent slit to allow the escape of hot air and the line that controls this opening, called a "ho hoo." It's the collapsing system that is different in the two. One has the rip panel at the top. When the rip line is pulled at touchdown, a large panel at the top of the balloon opens and the air escapes. Most balloons are the rip-panel type. The other system uses a dumping balloon. It has no opening at the top. On touchdown the envelope is released from the load plate. Seams near the mouth are opened. The envelope, without any weight attached to it, rises back into the air. The top or crown of the balloon is attached by rope to the gondola so when the free-flying envelope gets to "the end of its rope" it turns upside down and the hot air is released through the mouth and rip panels. When you see this the first time it looks as though the balloon is flying away, out of control.

PREPARATION FOR TAKEOFF

Ballooning is a team sport. You need at least three crew members who know what they are doing to inflate a rig. The first requirements are the right site and weather conditions. A football field is big enough for beginners to learn tethered flight but not big enough for free flights. A large pasture (about the size of three football fields) without obstructions is best. Because of the capricious nature of weather, it is foolhardy to make a flight without getting a weather report. From aviation weather stations you can get a report of surface winds and winds aloft. Local forecasts and the general weather pattern can be obtained from newscasts. A small helium-filled balloon released from the site will give you the best "reading" as to whether or not to proceed with the launch. If the test balloon goes straight up without any horizontal movement, there is a good chance that your flight will be becalmed. If the tester moves horizontally more than about eight mph (a matter of judgment; there's no way to gauge its actual speed), the flight should be canceled, especially for beginners. If the flight path is irregular, following an erratic course, it indicates gusty winds and thermals over the launch site. The best times of the day for launching are early morning and late afternoon if there is enough daylight left.

The launch site should be free of such obstructions as houses, power lines and trees. Crowds should be controlled and kept at a safe distance. A quick change of course or a sudden landing after takeoff could mean a problem for spectators.

Over hill and dale to Grandmother's house we go . . . if she lives downwind. Surface winds and winds aloft are usually not in the same direction. Winds aloft at varying altitudes are in varying directions. The balloon can be "steered" by taking advantage of this. To get to Grandmother's, the balloonist may have to do a lot of going up and down to find the most suitable wind.

With the unpredictability of weather, the balloonist should be ready to land when he encounters an approaching weather change. Fog, smog, lightning, rain, powerful gusts and heavy thermal activity are signals that a landing should be made soon. No wind at all can be just as much a problem if you're stalled over an area that it not suitable for landing. Balloons equipped with a maneuvering vent can make slight horizontal movements that will help in a tight situation. With a ground handling line, thrown to someone below, the balloon can be pulled to a safe landing area.

This all makes balloon flying sound haphazard. It's astonishing to a new flyer to discover how much control a good pilot *does* have. On my first flight our pilot asked my wife if she would like a cup of coffee. Not remembering a thermos being put aboard, I gave our pilot a quizzical look. His "answer" was a slow descent in a series of steps. He'd spotted a family having Sunday breakfast on their patio and in five minutes had the gondola hovering a few feet off the ground alongside the table. Sure enough, once the excitement of the ground-bound family abated, we were offered a cup of coffee. With cream and sugar to our liking, we were soon off to skim a ridge to pick leaves off the tops of the trees, which we made into a bouquet for my wife. Moments later we were aloft surveying the countryside. With farmland as far as the eye could see, we knew that our flight was whatever we wanted it to be. Low-level flight was the most fun. Everybody wanted to talk to us, and they did. We shouted back and forth, and if nobody could tell us exactly where we were, we'd go down and read the road signs.

THE FLIGHT

The burner for a hot-air balloon.

The assembly of a balloon is less than a half-hour job by a good team. On the left the gondola comes out of the van and the assembly begins. The frame is attached and then (below) the propane is secured. The hook-ups take only a few minutes. On the right the flow of gas is checked. All lines are clear for connection and the inflation can begin.

1. The gondola is laid on its side and the bag is attached to it and spread out on the ground...

2. The power fan is started and air will be blown into the bag...

3. The skirt is held clear and the cool air is blown into the envelope. This takes five minutes...

4. This is the time to get inside the balloon and inspect it as a pre-flight precaution...

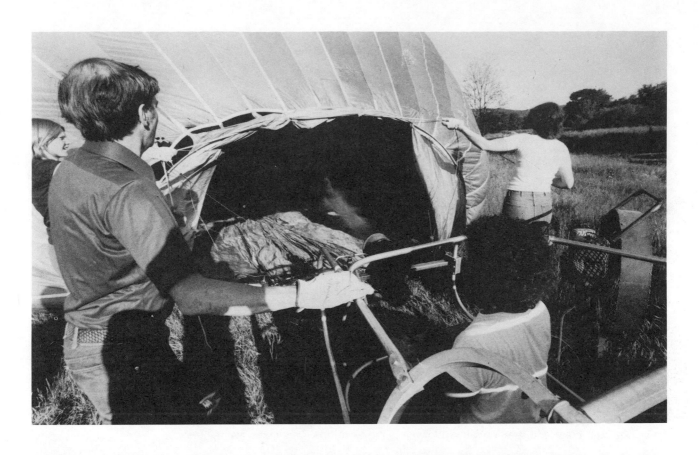

The burner is lighted and the heat applied, making sure that the flame does not touch the envelope. With the heat the balloon seems to come alive. Slowly it stands up and starts to tug to break free. Once the point of equilibrium is reached and passed, the flight begins.

Up . . . and away.

HOW SAFE IS CROSS-COUNTRY FLIGHT?

Safety in balloon flying is much the same as in all other flying . . . good judgment is required. Weather has already been mentioned. Many accidents happen in the air because pilots take the attitude, "I think the weather will be okay. Let's go."

Along with good judgment goes timing. Timing in the steering of a balloon is most critical. In a plane you move the stick and the response is instantaneous. In a hang glider you initiate a maneuver and it takes a second or so for the craft to respond. In a balloon it takes about twenty seconds for the change of direction to occur. In that way, a balloon is like a big elephant. On my first balloon flight this was demonstrated in a

Balloons come in all sizes and shapes. Some are more expensive than others. The one on the left has a simple gondola made of aluminum and canvas. It'll do the job just as well as the wicker basket. The load is called a basket when it's wicker, otherwise it's a gondola. Turn the page to see some different designs.

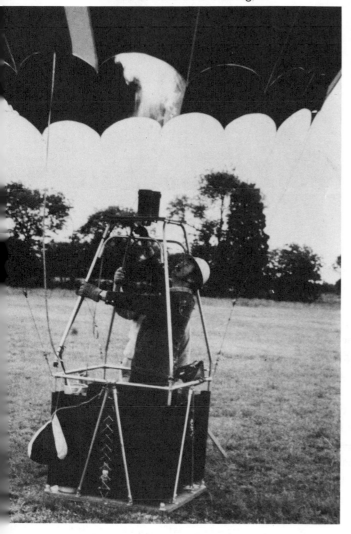

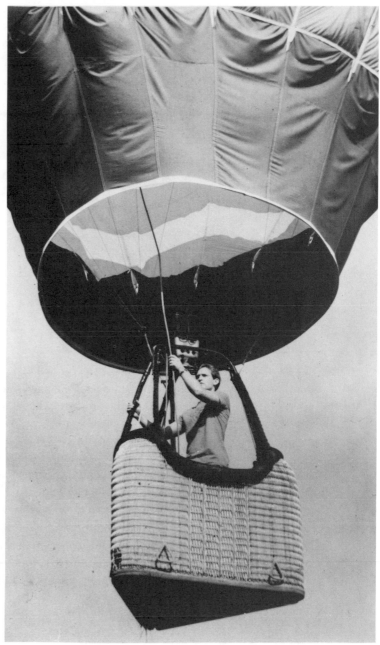

way that almost scared the wits out of me. We were traveling along a ridge at treetop level. Ahead I spotted a power line and pointed it out to our pilot. He'd seen it too, but seemed to be taking no diverting action. When I mentioned the situation he poured the heat to the bag, then calmly turned his attention elsewhere. My eyes stayed glued to those power lines. In spite of the head he'd applied to the envelope, our flight path was not changing—we were on a collision course. As the seconds passed, I felt an excitement swelling within me. At the instant when I could no longer contain my fear and was about to shout a warning, the gondola started to lift. Over the lines we floated, with plenty of altitude

Some of the shapes are fun.

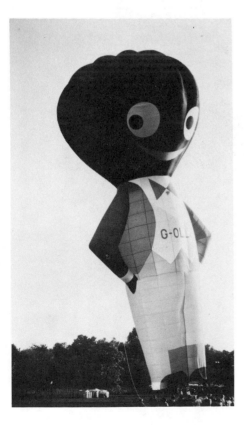

to spare. Noting my reaction, our pilot, Dick Behr, laughingly said, "The whole game is getting a feel of the response of the rig. Time and judgment are what it's all about. Why don't you try it?"

I took over control and within a few minutes was all over the sky. Ten minutes later I had the hang of the machine. Level flight was a matter of short bursts of heat. Longer bursts had us climbing. Descent was controlled by "stepping" down with very short bursts of heat. I had the elephant dancing, and she was following gracefully. I felt very much in control. It was all a matter of thinking twenty seconds ahead.

With that much under my belt, I asked Dick, "What happens if we run out of fuel or if we have a flameout?"

His answer was very reassuring. "We never let the first tank go completely empty. If there is a problem with the second tank we can always go back to the first one and have enough fuel in it to make a safe landing."

"What about a flameout?"

"It just doesn't happen if you pre-flight the ship. We don't fly in cold weather because at thirty degrees Fahrenheit and below, cold propane might not supply the necessary vapor pressure to force the liquid from the tanks into the fuel system to the burners. Also, we treat the tanks with methanol to make sure that the gas is not contaminated with water. Water will freeze and form ice within valves."

"Okay," I continued, "suppose in spite of all your pre-flight inspections and good maintenance you still have a fuel problem, a leak, or you do run out of gas. Then what?"

"If a leak develops anywhere in the system during flight, the main valve on the propane tank can be closed. Then, by opening all the other valves in the fuel system the pilot can use the main tank valve, opening and closing it to control the heat output to a safe landing."

"Okay, then what about an empty fuel tank?"

Dick laughed. "If you're that stupid, you've just changed sports."

"What does that mean?"

"You have an envelope, a bag of cooling air above you. It has a mouth opening at the bottom that is at least eight feet in diameter. As you descend, your balloon becomes a great big parachute and you go down at about the same rate of speed as a chutist. Tell me what kind of country is below you and I'll try to tell you how safe your landing will be. If you see at the last minute that you are on a collision course with some farmer's cow or his house, you can increase the rate of descent and land short of the obstacle by pulling the maneuvering vent line or, if close to the ground, by opening the deflation port."

For thousands of years man dreamed about getting up in the air. Those who first tried seemed to have had only half the dream. The other half was getting down . . . safely. History records every facet about the first ascent of de Rozier and d'Arlandes in 1783, including their dress, but only a scant word or two about their landing. What could they have thought, standing a mile over Paris?

A balloon landing can be a piece of cake or a hair-raising experience. It all depends on the wind. If you like excitement, you'll like shooting a landing. Once the area of landing is selected, the step-down descent is made. It's good procedure then to travel at a hundred feet or so above the ground, running horizontally until the exact landing spot is selected. Of course all those loose items have been secured and all crew members have been briefed. They must stand facing the direction of travel, in the center of the gondola, their knees slightly bent to absorb the shock. While on the horizontal flight a hundred feet above the ground, you can throw balls of crumpled paper overboard to give an indication of what the winds are doing closer to the ground. In normal smooth-air landings the final descent is made as the envelope cools. The blast valve is opened to level off before touchdown.

Problem landings develop when the wind is five to eight miles per hour or more. A run-on landing is made by shifting the crew weight to the side opposite the landing direction, opening the maneuvering vent and skidding the gondola on the ground. For winds above eight mph a longer landing distance will be needed and a low angle of approach made. All burners must be turned off before ground contact is made. The red deflation line must be pulled the instant before ground contact. With the deflation port open there is less chance that the balloon will climb back into the air. The deflation line should be snapped to the pilot's belt. In case he is thrown from the gondola he can then make sure the deflating operation is started.

Drag lines are not used in hot-air balloons, but a tether line can be dropped to someone on the ground to help bring them down. In the old days an anchor was thrown overboard. It skittered across the ground turning over outhouses and anything else in its path until it hooked something substantial.

LANDING THE ELEPHANT

GROUND CREWING...IT'S WORK BUT FUN

If you want to ride, you've got to earn it. Ballooning is a group sport. There is a lot of work involved with a piece of "machinery" this big. A well-trained crew will pay off. There are things to see to before the launch takes place. Are the fuel tanks full? Do the crew members have the right clothes, including gloves? Is the coffee made? Will food be needed? Are the charts and maps for the area available? Will survival gear be necessary? A good crew should be able to inflate a balloon in about ten minutes. Each member should know his job. Once the launch has taken place, one member of the ground crew should be responsible for seeing that all gear and tools left behind on the ground are retrieved.

BALLOONACY, SWISS STYLE

If there were only some kind of an award called "Bumbling Around in the Sky," I'd want to nominate myself as a candidate.

The narrative of why I should get the Sky Bumbling award is a long and tortuous one. It goes like this: A magazine editor said to me, "Why don't you fly across the Swiss Alps in a balloon?" It wasn't until I was sitting having a drink on a Swissair 747 that I stopped and asked myself, "What am I doing?" With the next drink I concluded if I was going to bumble I might as well do it in style ... and there is no better style than the Swiss.

It took five trains to get to my destination in Switzerland. The last one stood on its ear to get me to Mürren, a little town of only a few Swiss souls, five thousand feet up in the Alps. Picture-postcard quaint, it nestled in the shadows of three of the world's great peaks, the Eiger, the Mönch and the Jungfrau ... just like where Heidi lived. There were no automobiles, no motorcycles—even bicycles were outlawed. If you wanted to get to someplace in this village, you walked. I did, and promptly got lost. I was half hoping for one of those dogs with a keg on its neck to bumble along, or some charming Swiss maiden. With my luck, I got a nine-year-old boy to see me safely down the right path.

When I met Rolf Gross, my Swiss balloon pilot, in Mürren, he said the most wonderful thing to me about our flight. "Once we get aloft we will just go wherever the wind takes us."

I guess he didn't understand my English very well, because he just frowned when I answered, "No stick. No rudder. No nothing. That's real sky bumbling!"

The morning we were to take off, Rolf had tea for breakfast. John des Jardins, the other member of our crew, munched on toast and coffee. They were surprised that I packed in one Italian grapefruit, three kinds of Swiss cheese, two soft-boiled eggs, bacon, sweet rolls and cups of that sensational Swiss coffee. John asked if I thought I had to supply my own ballast. Rolf was more tactful and suggested that we'd have food along, and when we got to Italy we'd have a fine dinner. These guys didn't realize that I was an old hand at sky bumbling and was taking no chances.

Before sunrise, a professional crew started work on the rigging of the two balloons that were to make the flight from Mürren. The

Toblerone, piloted by British balloonist Jerry Turnbull, was to be off first, and we were to follow an hour later in the *Ajoie*.

The takeoff ritual is something only the Europeans could perform. Every citizen of Mürren, in his colorful Sunday best, stood in a circle around the takeoff site. There was an almost religious quality to the setting as Fred Dolder, president of the austere Spelterini Balloon Society, read in German the purpose of the flight and then a long safety checklist. He then raised his voice and said something in German that instantly transformed the scene into a festival. Four workers came forward to take hold of the wicker basket. With passengers aboard and the hydrogen bag straining to get on with things, the excess bags of sand that held the whole contraption on the ground were cut loose. The balloonmeister shouted, "Hands off!" The workers let go of the gondola. Nothing happened. "Hands on!" They held the basket, and more sand was removed. "Hands off!" and the *Toblerone* struggled like a drunken sailor. The crowd sensed that equilibrium would soon be achieved and the waving and shouting started. "Hands on!" was shouted and more sand was removed. When the next hands-off command was given a child could have sent the flying machine and its crew aloft. One more bag was removed and the command was "Hands off the *Toblerone*!" A wild cheer went up . . . even from me. Up went the balloon, and Roy Anderson, one of the crew in the basket, waved the bottle of champagne that every balloonist carries to drink when he touches down safely at the end of the flight. Some day that bottle may be found chilled in the snow on a Swiss mountaintop . . . unopened.

I'm glad that I saw all the details of that takeoff because when, an hour later, it was our turn to amble aloft, the activity was so frantic that I hardly remember my own pre-flight ceremony. But the moment the command "Hands off the *Ajoie*!" was given, an excitement swept over me that was unlike any I'd known. Standing in a flimsy wicker basket with my bulkheads, no windows, no fuselage, nothing between me and the wind, no force, no inertia, no thrust—this was real sky bumbling. There was no feeling of motion. It was as if we were standing still; the world below was moving, people dropping away, then the town becoming smaller, fields changing shape, dancing light playing all around. At the snow line a new world seemed to start, majestic yet treacherous. Ever so slowly we climbed up the sheer rock face of the Mönch; then the magnificence and grandeur of the Jungfrau dressed in stark white loomed at us.

At about fourteen thousand feet an uneasiness swept over me . . . almost a fear, and I couldn't shake the weirdness of the sensation. Was it fear? Then it struck me . . . oxygen! "Come now," I remember thinking, "I've flown my sailplane to over fourteen thousand feet without oxygen for short periods and it never got to me." I searched for the answer and found it—the absolute silence was something I had never encountered before. Soundlessness hurt my ears. We were part of the wind; the sky was completely silent, a quality not even

We waited nine days for the right weather. Before dawn on the day we went, the balloon was assembled on the green in the center of the Swiss village of Murren, one mile high in the Alps.

a wilderness can boast. The spell was broken by something to be remembered as long as there is memory: Out of the silence came the sound of a rushing river and the pounding of glacier water racing for sea level. Instantly it was gone. Waves of sound sang to us from the meadows below, ricocheting off the cliffs and precipices up through our silence.

Above it all, at the top of the world, for the first time I understood infinity . . . I could see it. Then, like the end of the first act, the curtain came down. We flew into cloud that materialized from nowhere. Silently, in the fluffy white lace, we hung in space, oriented to nothing but a wicker basket.

"Illegal as hell"—I heard the first words since takeoff from our pilot. Sure, we were illegal in the clouds, but there was absolutely nothing that we or anyone could do about it. That's bumbling in style . . . even to the point of having champagne on board. Once we cleared the clouds John and I seemed to bubble over with excitement as we came out of our state of euphoria. Sensing our pleasure, Rolf suggested we break out one of the extra bottles. But, like the crew of the *Toblerone*, we never got to drink our champagne.

The story of why we didn't taste the grape has its humor; the *Toblerone*'s story was a near tragedy. They were both taking place at the same time. Time had become meaningless and I couldn't have told if one hour or five had passed since we'd taken off. As John rummaged on the floor of our flying wicker hamper for the champagne, I glanced at my watch...exactly 1:33 P.M. At that very instant our aircraft radio came alive. John froze in his squatted position.

"Mayday, Mayday! This is the *Toblerone*," came the voice of Frank Hager blurting from the troubled balloon. "We struck an Alp at seven thousand feet. Going down. Spot us! Locate! Report us going down. No control!" The radio went dead.

Our champagne celebration ended before it began. The glorious, magnificent spectacle below suddenly became rugged, dangerous, vicious country. For an hour we strained our eyes, searching...once again our basket was silent...each man with his own prayers...we never had a chance, ambling helplessly on the wind, to find them.

When we crossed into the Italian Alps and the lake region, our spirits were lifted by the sheer splendor below. Lago Maggiore and its countryside were breathtaking. The rich blue water surrounded by forests in many shades of green was like a sapphire set in a brooch of jade. For me, the thrill of all times came over Lake Como. Below, thousands of feet below, four white fiberglass sailplanes, in formation, wingtip to wingtip, were crossing the lake. I almost fell out of our basket leaning over to shout down to them, "Good show! *Good show!*"

The hydrogen was brought up into the mountains by cable. It took about three hours to fill the bags. Great care was taken to prevent any sparks. We could wear no nylon.

Take-off seen from the ground...

On we drifted to Milano. The countryside became flat and dull . . . the heat of Italy oozed up to greet us. It was almost five P.M., so we prepared to land. We'd gone 110 miles and our ballast was getting low. There were fine fields all around, but unfortunately the wind shifted—and we were skimming only a few hundred feet above the ancient walled city of Romano di Lombardia. In our silence we could hear the excitement from below. We could see the kids running through the streets giving the alarm that a happening was about to happen.

A few ancient automobiles started up, motorcycle engines roared, bicycles wobbled to the city gate, baby carriages kicked up dust and the rest of the population ran under us, waving, shouting, screaming.

... take-off seen from the balloon.

They swarmed like bees from a hive and we were their flower. But they couldn't know that their flower was a bag of highly explosive hydrogen gas.

"Keep your eye on them!" shouted Rolf, and a little nervously he cursed the dying wind.

"Get this thing down!" I returned. "They're gaining on us." They came in all sizes and shapes, from babes in arms to crutch-hobbling farmers. We lumbered and bumbled down the last few feet ... touched gently ... then the trouble began.

What followed was unbelievable. The set could have been a scene from the last act of a well-tuned Italian tragicomic opera. Rolf Gross

The scenery was breathtaking. It took four hours to cross the Alps.

stood on the basket conducting in German to the chorus who could sing only in Italian. Then the ballet corps came onstage to do their festive dance around the balloon, which by this time was flopping around the ground like an oversized, well-stabbed heroine. Rolf tried to conduct them offstage.

If it had been tragic opera, the performers would have known the ending. The chorus and dancers didn't know that one cigarette or one spark would have turned the festive scene into a funeral march. The crowd scene, with all the theatrics of La Scala, lunged first from one side to the other to get a better look at the dying soprano. Like any good conductor, Rolf's hair was flying in all directions. I got in the act, jumped onstage and pranced around yelling, *"No fuma,"* whatever that was supposed to mean. Wherever I went, the chorus seemed to respond from the other side of our flopping heroine, who was taking too long to die. I threw my arms up over my head and hollered *"Boom!"* . . . up again they went and I boomed again. The actors loved it, they cheered. I was defeated. How could I tell them "explosion"? With nothing left to do, I bowed to their cheers and took their applause.

Then, as in all good Italian opera, onstage rushed the rotund hero. He dashed about in the resplendent uniform of the town's one policeman, and with a sweeping gesture of his hand he took our documents, written in German, and read them as if he understood them. No one was about to challenge his girth and dignity. Cast well in his part, with another theatrical sweep of his arm, he pushed the crowd back and brought forward youths to roll up the now-dead heroine, place her in a cart and push her offstage to a farmer's barn. And then came the realization of the real tragedy . . . in the packed balloon was our champagne. By the end of the last act I was thirsty.

Back in the Swiss Alps, Roy Anderson and Dr. Paul Potter, two members of the *Toblerone* crew, chopped glacier ice to suck. While we were taken to Romano by our officer hero, Carabiniere Marecillo, for a fine dinner and what would become a good rest in a quaint hotel, the crew of the *Toblerone* was preparing for a tough night ahead. Twenty-four hours later, when we were all back in Mürren drinking champagne, I got this story from the four of them.

Roy Anderson and Doc Potter told their part first. All seemed well with the flight at 15,700 feet over the Jungfrau, but an hour and a half later "The craft hit the fan," as Doc Potter expressed it. Suddenly they rose and fell like an elevator out of control. At 7,000 feet they were throwing everything they could get their hands on out of the basket . . . but to no avail. The basket, swinging like a pendulum, slammed into a rock face. Falling, they smashed into an ice slope and came to a halt. Pilot Turnbull sent Potter and Anderson out of the basket with a trail rope. The plan was to walk the partially filled balloon down the thirty-degree face of the glacier. Suddenly a violent wind flung the balloon and the two men still in the basket skyward. Potter and Anderson grabbed the drag line and lay on their backs digging their heels into the snow. The wind was too much for them and they were dragged down the chute of the glacier. Dragging and sliding, they were carried faster and faster all the way to the bottom of the ice field. Turnbull screamed for them to let go. From above in the basket, he could see that the ice field ended in a thousand-foot sheer drop. Potter and Anderson grabbed a rock in time and hung on. The balloon floated over the precipice, swung crazily, spewing things all over the landscape. In seconds the two, clinging to the rock to save their lives, lost sight of the balloon as it crashed below.

The first thing they did was work themselves, chain fashion, to the edge of the precipice. A thousand feet below, personal gear was strewn over hundreds of yards; the basket was on its side, with the deflated balloon hanging over another precipice. No sign of life. They were sure their fellow crewmen were dead.

In waist-deep snow, they climbed to find a way out, since they saw that going down was impossible. They made a big X in the snow and two rocks became their shelter, which they named the Plaza. Arm-in-arm they hugged each other all night. They tried not to sleep. Doc spent a few hours giving a lecture on gynecology; then Anderson, a professor, gave one on the economics of a society that was on the snow standard instead of the gold standard. They kept their spirits up, but Doc knew they had only three days left, dressed the way they were. They ate a snowball for breakfast.

When Turnbull screamed for the two on the glacier to let go of the drag line, he ordered Hager to lie down across the basket and brace himself with his feet and shoulders. Not knowing for sure whether the two men on the rope had been carried over the rock face or not, he braced himself across the basket on top of Hager. Hager said that they turned upside down and everything that was not tied fell out. They smashed down, taking a hard whack, and were airborne again, then fell over a second precipice.

At least they had some warm clothes and food. Both men were concerned for the two above and tried to climb up, but there was no way. They shouted and called every hour, but got no response. Hager took

The spectacle is Logo Maggiore.

the smashed radio and went to a mountain shelter they found three-quarters of a mile away. He spent all night repairing the radio, making an antenna out of the wire from the barograph. Turnbull, the survival expert, decided to climb down for help. He traveled until his path was blocked . . . he found no way down. Too exhausted to get back, he made a bed of grass and slept.

After a tough night, the warmth of the sun the next day was welcomed by all of them. Then, when the sun was high, they heard the drumming of the famous Swiss rescue helicopter. Hager's overnight radio repair shop service paid off. He talked them in. In minutes the helicopter plucked all of them off the mountain. The people of Mürren welcomed them with bouquets of flowers. A happy ending for everyone . . . except me.

I rushed back to the United States with my story and pictures of drifting aimlessly over the top of Europe. I sat in the editor's office and told him of my magnificent experience, hoping he'd sponsor me for the sky bumbling award. Then I did a very foolish thing. I told him about the crash of the *Toblerone*. He shook his head, then put his head down on his arms on his desk, still shaking it. Finally he got over the fit that had seized him and said, "You sure bumbled that assignment. You were on the wrong balloon."

YOU SHOULD KNOW... IF YOU ARE GOING TO TAKE UP BALLOONING

Ballooning, with only about a thousand licensed pilots, is the smallest of the air sports, but it's growing very fast. It does not require a license to be a member of a flight crew or to work on a ground crew. To become a pilot, the Federal Aviation Administration (FAA) has established these requirements:

You must be fourteen or older to be eligible for a student license and sixteen for a pilot's license. There is no upper limit on age, except that a rocking chair might be awkward in a gondola. No medical examination is needed. FAA has complete jurisdiction over the sport. To get a license that will allow you to carry passengers you must have a minimum of ten hours flying time plus ground training. A written examination is required. Two free flights of thirty-minute duration, one of which has to be above three thousand feet, plus a solo flight, are needed. In addition, there is a test flight with an approved FAA inspector.

The specific flight and ground requirements set by the FAA can be obtained by writing and requesting "FAA Regulations, Part 31—Airworthiness standards: Manned Free Balloons" and "FAA Regulations, Part 61—Certification, Pilot and Flight Instructors." The address is FAA, 800 Independence Ave., S.W., Washington, D.C. 20591. If you have no personal contacts in the sport you should write for information to the Balloon Federation of America (BFA), 806 Fifteenth St., N.W., Suite 610, Washington, D.C. 20005. They are the official clearing-house for ballooning in this country and can put you in touch with people in your area who are active in the sport. There is a choice of ways to obtain a ballooning license. There are formal schools which will cost a thousand to fifteen hundred dollars for the instruction, use of the equipment, flight fees, and ground crew with chase car equipped with radio. The other way is club operations, which are cheaper than the schools.

Balloon clubs and partnerships have sprung up all over the country. Of course the initial cost varies, but it will cost about seven hundred fifty to a thousand dollars to join a club; flights will then cost the price of fuel for the balloon and gas for the chase car. The initial cost is high in ballooning, but once that is paid and the skill of piloting is learned it's very inexpensive.

Flight training usually starts with tethered flight, where vertical control is learned; it's a feel you must achieve since there is a lag between the time a control is initiated and the balloon responds. At the same time you will be trained in ground work, learning to assemble and deflate the balloon. Safety and weather will be studied; they are very important in balloon flying. You will become a part of a team. Free flight will be the next step, and if you are an excellent student, soloing could come as early as the fifth or sixth flight.

A three-place balloon will cost from sixty-five hundred to ten thousand dollars, but that will include everything needed. Two-place units are a little cheaper.

With care, a balloon will last a long time. The first of the modern ripstop envelopes, built in 1961, is still flying. The nylon can't take rough ground handling. Sharp objects will tear it. The balloon should be stowed out of the sunlight while not in use. The balloon must be inspected after each twenty-five hours of flight, and the FAA requires inspection at one hundred hours or once a year, whichever comes first. Sport balloons are classified by size, ranging from AX−1 to AX−10. A−6, −7, and −8 are the common sizes and will comfortably carry two to four people; these are about sixty to seventy feet tall and have a volume of between fifty and sixty thousand cubic feet.

The FAA requires that the balloon be equipped with a compass, altimeter, a rate-of-climb meter (it's best for this to be a variometer because of its quick response) and a pyrometer, which is to measure the internal air temperature at the top or crown of the envelope. Aircraft radio is used to stay in touch with the chase car. Many use CB for communications . . . it's a lot cheaper.

Competition flying in ballooning is very imaginative. The best-known event is the "hare and hounds": The leader, the hare, takes off alone and after a short interval the pack, the hounds, follows. When the leader lands, the rest of the pack follow. The one that lands the closest to the "hare" is the winner. Another popular event requires a barograph (a recording barometer). Before the event, the committee declares the trace they want on the barograph. They will specify that after takeoff the balloon should be flown at two thousand feet for twenty minutes, then at three thousand feet for thirty minutes, back down to fifteen hundred feet for another given time period and then a landing. The barograph trace that comes closest is the winner. Scaven-

The contrast of these two pictures is so
typical of the sport. This is a contest.
They appear to be very relaxed affairs
but, as the picture on the left indicates,
balloon competition is very exciting.

ger hunts are also popular. The balloon takes off and lands as close as possible to certain specified objects. A crew member runs to retrieve the "thing," then they are off again. The team that collects the most specified items is the winner.

In many ways ballooning is the most social of all the silent sports. It takes teamwork, work on the ground and, since two or three people can fly at one time, it's great sport after launch for the ground crew to follow the balloon across country. When the chase vehicle and balloon meet, passengers may be exchanged.

If you are seriously considering this sport you should join the Balloon Federation of America; membership is ten dollars a year. Their publication, *Ballooning*, is a very handsome magazine that comes out quarterly. It covers every aspect of the sport and is an excellent source of information. It reports on major happenings around the world, contest events, current events in the sport.

Good information can be obtained about the sport by writing to the four leading manufacturers: The Balloon Works, Rhyne Aerodrome, RFD 2, Statesville, North Carolina 28677; Cameron Balloons, 3600 Elizabeth Rd., Ann Arbor, Michigan 48103; Don Riccard Balloons, P.O. Box 1902, Newport Beach, California 92660; and Raven Industries, Inc., P.O. Box 1007, Sioux Falls, South Dakota 57101.

Buoyant Flight is a bimonthly magazine put out by the Lighter Than Air Society, 1800 Triplett Blvd., Akron, Ohio 44306. It carries interesting articles not only on hot-air ballooning, which is what the BFA *Ballooning* covers, but also on all types of lighter-than-air aviation.

The Wind Drifters Ballooning Club, 2814 Empire Ave., Burbank, California 91563, publishes an *FAA Examination Guide*, a helpful tool for studying for the written examination necessary for getting the pilot's license. It also publishes a good book called *Introduction to Club Ballooning*.

A well-written book covering every phase of the sport for both the beginner and the practicing balloonist is *The Balloon Book*: *A Complete Guide to the Exciting Sport* by Paul Fillingham, published by McKay. It's well illustrated.

Other good books: *The Complete Ballooning Book* by Will Hayes, published by World Publications, Mountain View, California, is very informative. *Bags Up!* by Kurt Stehling, Playboy Press, is enjoyable reading about some wild exploits and entertaining tales of ballooning history.

3
SOARING

There is no doubt in my mind that soaring is the most fulfilling way to fly. It satisfies the wish and dream of the kite flier. The balloonist is only a spectator in the sky, having to accept what the winds provide. The sky diver has only one way to go—down. The hang glider is desperately seeking the hawk's control, which the soaring pilot has mastered. Sailplanes can outfly the bird in every way, climb faster, higher, go farther and do aerobatics. Granted that each sport has its own thrill, I'm convinced that the sense of accomplishment is greatest in soaring.

Feature stories in the news on soaring are misleading. The reporter takes a demonstration ride and as a spectator writes about what he sees—which is spectacular; what he feels—which is sensational; and then from the back seat he composes poetic prose about being a bird and the glory of it all. If the truth be known, the soaring pilot spends very little time lolling in poetic serenity. The only poem he knows is:

Get high.
Stay high.

Soaring is like playing chess. It takes a lot of concentration and constant planning ahead. There are infinite options, but unlike chess you have to be making your moves constantly. The opponent is Mother Nature, and to checkmate her is to find and use the invisible fuel that she can provide; the game is to unravel her secrets. To win is to fly a sailplane a few hundred miles cross-country. The soaring pilot flies an airworthy, stable, highly maneuverable machine. Soaring is an intellectual game and it is played on each flight. It's a game of calculating, planning and guessing to outwit gravity. That's what man has been trying to do for centuries.

The uninitiated wonder how in the world it's possible to fly a plane without any visible means of power. One way or the other, they phrase their doubts by asking, "How safe is soaring?" It's an extremely safe sport, as the record shows. It's as safe as flying a commercial airliner and safer than driving the car to the airport. It's so safe that the FAA, which governs all flight, allows kids of fourteen to solo, and that's two years before they may drive a car in most states.

The question of safety arises out of fear. We all seem to be afraid of things we don't understand. Learning the principles of soaring flight will quickly dispel the fears, for we've not only learned to overcome gravity by using it, but we're doing it very well. While this was in the writing, a soaring pilot broke the existing world record and flew a distance of more than a thousand miles. Altitude flights have been made to forty-six thousand feet, and that's higher than commercial airliners can go. It's taken many years to get this far, and it hasn't always been this safe.

THE PAST

There have been stories of flying from the time records were kept, but until the eleventh century all flights were reported secondhand. In Babylon, stone etchings told about Etana's flight aboard a giant eagle.

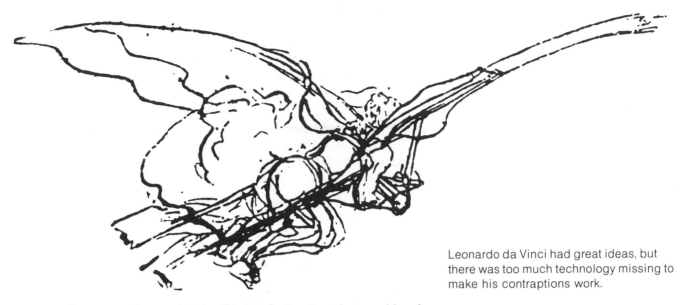

Leonardo da Vinci had great ideas, but there was too much technology missing to make his contraptions work.

His mission was to fly to a foreign land to find a plant that would make the women of his village bear children. Somehow he got mixed up with a woman named Ishtar, the goddess of birth. She threw him off his eagle before the day of parachutes. There were earlier stories from China about Ki-kung-shi, who invented a flying chariot, so Etana's tale may not be the first about flight—but it may be the first about Women's Lib.

Everybody got into the flying act, or at least that's how the stories went. Kai Kawus, a Persian king, had four hungry eagles pull his throne by having the birds frantically trying to reach slabs of meat impaled on spears ahead of them. Later it was said that Alexander the Great became a flyboy, doing the same thing as the Persian, except with winged griffins. The Greeks had the winged horse, Pegasus, and the famous story of Daedalus and Icarus, who fashioned wings of feathers and wax only to fly too close to the sun. Mercury was the Roman representative. Every culture and every society had its story but they were all hard to believe because they were secondhand. In the eleventh century we find the first believable story because it has its own firsthand quote by the pilot. Oliver of Malmesbury, an English monk-mechanic-mathematician, said, "Ie causet to mak ane pair of wingus." Whereupon he flew a furlong, broke both legs and announced, before the ambulance arrived, that he had failed because he forgot to attach the tail to the "hinder parte."

From the time man was first interested in kites, nothing significant took place leading to heavier-than-air flight until the early 1800s when George Cayley set down the principle that air must be forced over wings to create lift. It took a hundred years for his principle to be put into practice. Leonardo da Vinci had great ideas, but there was too much technology missing to make his contraptions work. Roger Bacon's contribution to flight was a vague remark: "Instruments to flie withal, so that one sitting in the middle of the instrument, and turning about an engine, by which the wings being artificially composed may beate the ayre after the manner of a flying bird." Of all the brains around Europe

Captain LeBris and his passenger.

during those hundred years, Isaac Newton was the only one who came close. His Third Law of Motion (to every action there is opposed an equal reaction) is today's theory of flight, and he even knew it; he prophesied: "This is the principle which will enable mankind in later centuries to undertake flights to the stars."

Cayley chickened out and never had the nerve to try his principles, but he constructed a glider that carried a ten-year-old boy a few yards down a slope. After his writings there was a rash of ideas that step by step led to Kitty Hawk. One idea that wasn't really in the mainstream of progress but must be told is that of a Frenchman, Captain LeBris.

The old sea captain had stood on the bridge so long watching the albatross effortlessly fly by his ship that he got the idea he could do it. Had da Vinci been a sailor and watched the soaring birds instead of the flappers, he might have done better than the sailor. LeBris built a ninety-two-pound artificial "bird" with a fifty-foot wing span. He put his contraption, which looked like an albatross, in a cart, hired a driver and headed down the road into a ten-mile-an-hour wind. Standing in the bird, LeBris screamed speed-up instructions to the driver. When all was ready, by a series of levers, he varied the inclination of the wings and achieved lift-off. At the propitious moment, horse at full gait, driver screaming to the horse, captain screaming to the driver, ropes were released and up flew the bird, captain and all. One hitch. The rope lassoed the driver. The bird soared to three hundred feet, carrying a cheering, triumphant sailor and a screaming, terrified peasant. Another first in aviation: the first non-paying passenger.

The 1890s brought a great deal of flurry in the aviation "market" on both sides of the Atlantic. The real breakthrough came when a German, Otto Lilienthal, put Cayley's theories into practice. He worked on the problem for thirty years before he made and flew his first cotton-covered, bamboo-framed glider. Making flights of over three hundred feet in his forty-four-pound machine, he was the first to understand the use of gravity as his motor power and of surface controls for stability.

Otto Lilienthal, the father of aviation, was the inspiration for the Wright brothers. (bottom)

Did John Montgomery's glider fly before Lilienthal's? Dan Maloney made a dazzling flight in it by being launched from a hot-air balloon.

During the five years that he experimented he made more than two thousand flights. He learned to turn, rise higher than his starting point and glide straight to a landing. He was the first to actually soar. In 1896, while experimenting on flight stability, he was killed. He earned his place in the history of flying as the father of aviation, and the soaring award in his name is the most coveted prize.

In the year of Lilienthal's death, Octave Chanute, a railroad engineer, gave up his construction engineering to turn his attention to heavier-than-air flight. He made thousands of flights along the shores of Lake Michigan, but his great achievement was his book, *The Progress of Flight.*

Chanute was the first to predict that motor power would not be necessary for long flights. "The machine," he wrote, "would be so constructed that the position of the center of gravity would give the apparatus a downward inclination. With such a machine one would circle like a bird, rise spirally like a bird and soar in any direction."

Backyard contraptions were built all over America and Europe with little or no success except for one pioneer, John Montgomery. He claimed that he flew his glider in Southern California before Lilienthal started flying. In 1883, it's claimed, Montgomery flew six hundred feet on the arid border of Mexico. The world didn't really hear about Montgomery until 1905 when he teamed up with Dan Maloney, a brave young man who became the test pilot for Montgomery's creations. They launched their flying machines from hot-air balloons. The first launch was from eight hundred feet. Later drops from four thousand feet created a sensation in the press and demonstrated remarkable control. A newspaper account stated:

In the course of the descent the most extraordinary and complex maneuvers were accomplished—spirals and circling turns were executed with ease and grace almost beyond description, level flight with and against the wind, figure-eight evolutions performed without difficulty, and hair-raising dives with speeds, as estimated by eye-witnesses, of over sixty-eight miles an hour, and yet after a flight of approximately eight miles in twenty minutes the machine was brought to rest upon a previously designated spot, three-quarters of a mile from where the balloon had been released, so lightly that the aviator was not even jarred, despite the fact that he was compelled to land on his feet, not on a special alighting gear.

Chanute characterized that flight as "the most daring fete [sic] ever attempted." Even today the flight of that kitelike contraption would seem spectacular, but such events didn't prepare the public for the Wright brothers. Few were ready to dare believe that man could fly, and Maloney's death on a subsequent flight reinforced their doubt.

THE BROTHERS WRIGHT

Every schoolboy knows what happened at Kitty Hawk. The Wright brothers started their own study of the dynamics of manned flight the year Lilienthal was killed. Wilbur wrote, "We had taken up aeronautics merely as a sport. We reluctantly entered upon the scientific side of it." They invented the wind tunnel to observe the flow of air over their wing designs. By 1902 they were making successful glider flights of more than six hundred feet. But gliding flight became predictable, and a year later, on a cold December day, they killed all interest in gliding with their first powered flight.

The country was not ready for any kind of flying success, power or gliding. It was no more than a curiosity in the United States, but Europe acclaimed the Wright brothers. Finally Teddy Roosevelt instructed the Army to investigate the new flying gadget. Then World War I gave power flying a premature impetus that left soaring still further in the shadows. After the war, only a handful saw the commercial value of power flying, and then it was left in the hands of the daredevils. Gliding died, except in Germany. Because of the Versailles Treaty, the only way Germans could fly was without power. In 1920 they held their first postwar soaring meet. In 1921 Orville Wright's 1910 duration flight record of nine and three-quarters minutes was broken twice. Herr Hirth flew his glider for twenty-one minutes, and the Americans, who were doing their flying on bathtub gin, couldn't have cared less.

Flying never really took hold in America until Lucky Lindy became a national hero. After that every kid wanted to become an aeroplane pilot. It still didn't do much for gliding. Two events took place in Germany that changed that picture. When Lindbergh was flying the Atlantic, Messrs. Lippisch and Kronfeld were involved in a less spectacular project. They were inventing the variometer, which Kronfeld then used to soar up to six thousand feet and go ninety miles cross-country. The variometer allowed even an inexperienced pilot to find and stay within the confines of a thermal. The glider would now become a sailplane and be able to both ascend and descend.

Up until this time gliding was a matter of flying close to a ridge, and after a while that becomes boring. Now, with thermal flight, the bird was free. Interest in the sport was renewed, and in this country Elmira, New York, became the soaring capital. The same Wolf Hirth who had broken the Orville Wright record in 1921 came to America and in 1930 made the first soaring cross-country flight. From Harris Hill in Elmira, he flew about forty miles to Appalachin, New York.

In 1930 Charles and Anne Lindbergh both took up soaring. The movement was begun. National contests were held and by 1932 the Soaring Society of America was formed. In 1934 Richard du Pont, of the well-known industrial family, flew 154 miles to establish a new world distance record.

It's not the purpose here to trace flight history completely. Our purpose is to show that from Babylonian times when Etana "flew" in search of a child-bearing potion until recently, man's thoughts have been about the "controlled flight of birds." You come along at a time when it's no longer a fantasy, it's a fact. It's safe and as magnificent as all our predecessors dreamed it would be.

When we discussed lift in the kite chapter it was rather easy to understand because we were talking about flying an object that weighed only a few pounds at most. Sailplanes weigh anywhere from three hundred to two thousand pounds plus the weight of one, two or three people. How is it possible without a motor?

HOW DOES IT REALLY FLY?

Weight, which was a major concern at one point in the development of flight, is relatively unimportant today. Lilienthal's birds weighed forty-four pounds. Today pilots carry as much as 350 pounds of water in their wings, as extra weight, to make sailplanes fly more efficiently.

A sailplane flies by the same principles as an airplane. There are four factors that must be considered to understand flight: lift, gravity, drag and thrust. We have explained lift. If you don't know what gravity is, here is a simple experiment that will teach you: Drop a hammer on your foot. You will encounter drag, or resistance, by putting your hand out the window of a moving car. Thrust is the power produced by the engine. To make powered flight, the propeller's thrust cancels out the drag; the propeller also forces air over the wings producing lift, which cancels out gravity. Get a balance between these four forces and you have power flight.

Modern sailplanes can make speed runs of over 150 mph. They carry over 300 pounds of water for ballast.

Now eliminate the motor, as we do in a sailplane, and we'll produce flight with the three forces by using gravity as our thrust. In the airplane, gravity, or weight, was considered a useless force that had to be overcome. Now it becomes our friend. It's the force that overcomes drag (the wind resistance of the plane itself as it passes through the air). As gravity makes the sailplane move through the air, air is forced over the flying surfaces and lift is produced, just as if a propeller were forcing the air over the wing.

To accomplish this, the nose of the sailplane is pointed down slightly in order to obtain the necessary speed to allow the flow of air to do exactly what it does for the airplane. That means the sailplane is always in a descending attitude. It's always gliding down in what is called its own "relative wind," the air that immediately surrounds it.

HOW DOES A SAILPLANE STAY UP FOR HOURS IF IT'S ALWAYS DESCENDING?

A simple experiment will explain how a glider can descend to produce flight and still climb. Sail a paper plane across a room in still air and its flight will be a continuous descent. Gravity brings it down but the thrust, produced by the throwing hand, is forcing the air surrounding the paper wings (relative wind) to make lift. The descent is gradual; that is gliding flight. Fly the same paper plane over a campfire and it will glide down until it gets into the rising warm air over the fire; then it will climb. As it climbs it is still under the influence of gravity. It's still descending in the immediate air around it and producing flight, but the whole mass of air over the fire is rising. The rate of sink of the paper plane is not as fast as the rate of climb produced by the column of rising hot air . . . so up it flies.

Think of it this way. Walk down an escalator that is going up. If you walk down more slowly than the escalator is going up, you will be walking down but will actually be going up. Your walking down is similar to the plane's gliding flight. The escalator is similar to the updrafts in the atmosphere that enable a glider to soar.

The sailplane has the same controls as an airplane, and has even better maneuverability. The only difference is that an airplane carries its fuel for sustained flight and a sailplane has to find it to use it.

The ailerons turn the plane by banking it, and the rudder helps the plane make the turn efficiently. The elevator controls the up-and-down attitude or speed. Sailplanes have another feature. They have either dive brakes, spoilers or flaps, enabling them to make descents with precision by partially destroying the lift of the wing. With this control a good pilot can land a sailplane on a tablecloth set out on the landing strip.

WHAT KIND OF CONTROL DOES A SAILPLANE HAVE?

Much to the surprise of most people, the sailplane cockpit is very sophisticated. The panel has variometer to measure lift for varying conditions both weak and strong, a compass, altimeter, air-speed indicator, accelerometer to give G-load reading, radio, oxygen regulator and a turn-and-bank which has to be removed for contest flying. On the seat is a circular computer that has the plane's performance figured in, two competition cameras sitting next to the control stick. The handle on the control stick is for the landing-gear wheel brake. The retractable landing-gear handle is to the right. On the left the handles are for the trim, for the dive brakes and for the flaps.

The Ailerons

The ailerons are movable flaps on the outer trailing edge of the wing. They are moved and controlled by the stick in the cockpit. When the stick goes left the right aileron goes down and the left one goes up. The ship banks left because the downed aileron on the right wingtip causes that tip to get more lift. Up it goes. The left aileron, in the up position, causes less lift to that side, so down it goes. The up wingtip, with more lift, flies faster—you could say it flies around the lower tip—so the plane is banked and turning. But a strange thing happens. That raised wingtip with more life is traveling at a faster speed, so it causes more drag on that side. The extra drag on the upwing side causes the nose of the plane to yaw toward the upwing direction. That means that the plane is not making a clean turn but going a little sideways, a defect in the turn. This produces a lot of drag from the fuselage and will cause unnecessary loss of altitude.

Rudder

The defect in the turn is corrected by the rudder. It solves the yawing problem. The rudder, connected to the vertical fin, operated by foot pedals, swings the nose of the plane in the direction of the turn, compensating for the yaw. The relative wind (the air immediately around the plane) then flows cleanly over the surfaces and drag is reduced. Many people have a misconception about the rudder. They see it move like the rudder on a boat and assume that it steers the plane. It does not. The rudder assists the wings only by making the turn "clean."

Flying clean, without excess drag, is important and can be judged from the yaw string.

The cheapest instrument a soaring pilot has is a yaw string. It's an eight-inch piece of yarn attached at one end to the canopy. It shows if the plane is flying cleanly. No matter what maneuver the plane makes, if the yaw string is not pointing directly back toward the center of the plane, a correction of the rudder or aileron will have to be made.

The ailerons.

Elevator

The elevator is connected to the horizontal stabilizer and is controlled by the stick. Push the stick forward and the elevator goes down. This changes the angle the plane points, called angle of attack. Stick forward, the sailplane descends and speed is increased. Back pressure on the stick will bring the nose up and reduce speed.

How much maneuverability does a sailplane have? Try this. Stick forward. Wings level. Dive. Slowly put back pressure on the stick. You're starting a loop.

HOW DO YOU GET INTO THE AIR?

Lilienthal launched by jumping off a mound of dirt a hundred feet high. Montgomery had his glider carried aloft by balloon and then cut free. Everything from slingshots to shoving the craft off cliffs has been tried. Today there are three acceptable methods: winch, auto tow and air tow. Airplane tow is used in this country far more than the other two

Rudder (top left). Spoilers or dive brakes destroy the lift over a section of the wing, making controlled descents possible (top right)

Preflight check of the elevator is a most essential safety procedure. (bottom)

The safest and most efficient launch of a sailplane is done with an airplane. Once aloft, the sailplane either flies above or below the area of turbulence produced by the propeller. The sailplane in the picture on the left is on low tow. Below, the sailplane is above the prop-wash. High tow is considered safest. If the rope breaks on low tow, it could spring back and fall on the sailplane's controls and jam them.

Either the tow plane or the sailplane pilot can release the rope. The power plane releases only if there is a problem. On the right, the break is being made by the sailplane on high tow. Once separated, the sailplane makes a climbing turn to the right, and the tow dives and turns left. That quickly puts as much space as possible between them.

The sailplane leaves the ground first. It stays low and hugs the ground to make it easier for the two to get into the air. Once they both climb out, the sailplane flies formation until they reach release altitude.

methods. It's the safest means of getting into the air and the most flexible. Whereas a good winch or auto tow might produce a launch to fifteen hundred feet, the airplane can take you to any altitude and drop you off in lift.

The air tow is done with a one-hundred-fifty-foot polyethylene rope that is connected to the tail of the tow plane and to a hook built into the glider. It can be released by either pilot, but the tow pilot releases only if there is an emergency.

Air tow is formation flying. The airplane is positioned on the ground a rope's length ahead of the sailplane. Both planes are hooked up. The tow plane inches forward until the line has tension. Then the wing of the sailplane is lifted off the ground. Since the sailplane has only one wheel, it must be balanced by the wing boy. When the sailplane's wings are held parallel to the ground, all is ready. The tow pilot hits the throttle on signal and away they go. The wing boy runs as fast as he can, holding the wings parallel until there is enough air speed for it to support itself. Within seconds the sailplane is airborne. Its large wing has much more lift than the airplane's, therefore it's off the ground first. The sailplane is flown close to the ground as the airplane taxis, gathering speed for its own takeoff. Once both are in the air, the sailplane stays on the tow plane's tail . . . in perfect formation.

There are two acceptable tow positions. The tow plane's propeller throws back a band of turbulent air called wash. One towing position is above the wash and the other below. The safest position is above the wash. The reason: In case of a rope break, the rope can't spring back and fall on the sailplane if it's in the high position.

Formation flying is continued to the desired altitude. When the sailplane pilot is ready, he releases by opening his hooking device. Immediately he turns to the right, to swing the sailplane away from the released rope. The tow plane turns left on release, carrying the dangling rope back to the airport for the next tow.

It never fails. As many times as I've landed a sailplane in some farmer's field, he, or one of the throng who have come to witness the happening, asks, "What's the matter, did the wind give out?" Popular belief is that sailplanes fly on the wind. Wind is the horizontal flow of air. Sailplanes climb on updrafts, or vertical movement of air. There are four updraft conditions in the atmosphere that are used extensively by the soaring pilot: ridge lift, thermals, mountain or lee waves and sea breeze fronts. Wind sheer and cold fronts are also used, but not usually by the beginner.

WE'RE OFF TOW. WHAT REALLY KEEPS THE SAILPLANE UP?

Ridge Lift

Ridge lift is produced by a strong wind blowing against the face of an obstruction, such as a mountain ridge, so that the air is deflected vertically. The sailplane is flown to the windward side and flies on the cushion of air that is deflected up.

In 1901, before they ever flew, Wilbur Wright wrote that it would be possible to fly on the front of a hill if the wind blew with sufficient force. When the Wright brothers did it they established a nine-minute record that stood for more than ten years. Today, duration records are not kept. Sixty hours had been recorded when it became evident that the record had nothing to do with skill. It became a contest to see who could stay awake the longest, since the plane would stay aloft as long as the wind blew to produce ridge lift.

Ridge flying is an excellent place for the beginning pilot to learn how to fly and get a lot of time and experience in the air. It's also a fantastic means of going great distances. If the wind is steady and the ridge a few hundred miles long, it can be flown in both directions . . . out and return. Ridge flights of over a thousand miles have been made.

It's a sensational experience since at times the wingtip is only yards from the trees.

Ridge lift flying is great sport. You can stay up as long as the wind blows. It's possible to fly with a wing almost touching the trees. This picture is a perfect explanation of how a sailplane stays up for hours if it's always descending. The plane is flying along at a very fast speed, but its flight is level. It is descending in the rising air. The descent produces the thrust needed to pass the air over the wings to produce lift. The lift keeps it flying level, although it appears to be going down. If the speed were reduced, the lift would make the plane rise. If the lift were reduced (ridge lift not as strong), the speed would be reduced to maintain level flight.

Thermal Flight

A thermal is a rising body of warm air. Thermals are capricious and, being invisible, are hard to find and even harder to describe. They exert tons of energy, but since we can't see any work being done by the thermals we tend to ignore them. Only painters, photographers and lovers seem to pay any attention to them, and then they only admire the signature the thermal leaves in the sky, the fluffy cumulus cloud.

Thermal flying is actually powered by the sun and can take place during daylight hours any place, be it in the Arctic or at the equator. The sun heats the earth at different rates according to the makeup of its surface. A field of dark soil will absorb heat more than a wooded area. The sun does not heat the air directly. The air is warmed from the ground heat. Since the ground is at different temperatures according to its makeup, the air above it will be heated unevenly. Air over the warmest areas will rise. You might think of the warmed air as a bubble breaking away from the cooler air that surrounds it. As it goes up, the surrounding cool air rushes in to take its place. It, in turn, gets warmed by the ground and up it goes, too. Thermals are known to work for hours at a time, producing a column of rising air.

The principle of soaring flight is to find a thermal. Locate its core and stay in its confines by circling tightly. As it goes up it will take the sailplane up with it. The rate of climb can be from a few feet per minute to an astonishing two thousand feet per minute. Five-hundred-feet-per-minute thermals are common in the eastern United States and thousand-footers are common in the Southwest. A ten-thousand-foot climb is not uncommon. It's no problem on a good day for a sailplane to outclimb a small power plane. There are some days when it's just a matter of getting up in the air and there is lift everywhere. To get down it's necessary to use the spoilers or dive brakes. Then there are days where you have to work hard just to stay aloft.

Finding the Thermal   One of the instruments you will carry in your panel is a variometer. It measures rate of climb or descent instantly. This is very important for helping you find thermals.

Let's assume you are at three thousand feet. You are gliding along at fifty-five miles per hour, which we'll assume is the best glide speed for your particular sailplane. It's known as the best L/D (lift/drag) speed and is the speed at which you will be able to cover the greatest distance while searching for thermals.

Cumulus Clouds or Wet Thermals   If there is moisture in the air as the thermal leaves the ground, it will carry the water vapor up with it. As it rises, it will cool and when it gets high enough it will condense and produce a cumulus cloud. You won't be able to see it rise but you will see it start to condense. First a wisp will appear. Then it will grow as more moisture rises and condenses. In a matter of minutes a full-fledged cloud will be formed. The problem is, when you see a

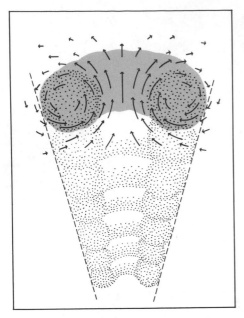

The artist's concept of the thermal is like an ice-cream cone. The sailplane when flying near the "cones" will experience a buffet, and a wing tip will be bumped up. There is lift, a thermal, in the direction of the lifted wing. The pilot turns into it.

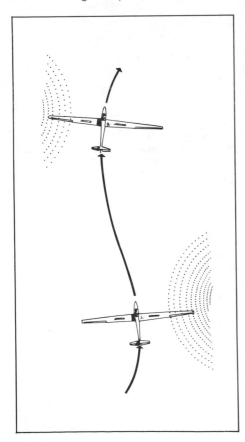

wisp in the sky, is the cloud forming or is it dissipating? You have to watch it to see if it's building or not. If the cloud is building, fly for it. Get under it. Take note of the wind direction. A thermal will be blown downwind. Try to intercept the "column" of updraft that starts on the ground and is angling up on the wind to the wisp.

Here is the way you fly a thermal. As you glide along, hold the plane steady and be ready for a wingtip to lift. Your fifty-foot wings cover a lot of sky and the tip might be lifted by the edge of a thermal. As you get close to a thermal, the variometer will start to inch up. As soon as you feel any turbulence or one wingtip is lifted, turn your plane in the direction of the lifted top. Start to circle. Slow the plane down to the "minimum sink speed"—at this speed you will lose less altitude. Remember, you are always descending in a glider. The faster you go, the faster you will descend. So when you are in lift you want to go at the slowest possible speed, without stalling. The slower you can circle in the confines of the thermal the faster you will climb. Remember the paper plane over the open fire? The slower the paper plane is going while passing over the fire, the higher it will go.

Your variometer will show you where you are in relation to the thermal. Let's say you are circling to the right. As you go around your vario goes up for one quarter of the turn, then goes down. Move the pattern of the circle, the next time around, toward the area of lift. If the vario shows "up" for half the circle, move over to the left and search until the variometer reads a steady up through the full circle. Now you have cored the thermal. Hold that place in the thermal and keep adjusting your position so that you get the highest readings all the way around the circle. Ride it up until it peters out. Fly out of the thermal and increase your speed to the best L/D; glide off and start the search for the next thermal.

Dry Thermals If there is no moisture in the atmosphere the thermals will be "dry." No cumulus clouds will appear to signal the lift. To find updrafts under these conditions, you have to know the ground conditions that produce thermals. Here are examples of the sort of things you have to know about: the type of soil, the cover, the terrain and the wind.

According to its makeup, areas absorb heat at different rates; color is a basic factor. White reflects the sun's rays without heating the ground or the air above it; dark earth absorbs the heat and radiates it to the air. If dark ground is caused by dampness, then it's cool and not going to be a thermal maker. If a dark field sits high on a knoll and is drained well, it could be a good thermal producer, but if a brisk wind is blowing across the knoll, the air above it won't have time to get warm, so it might have to be ruled out. Plowed fields are a good source because the furrows provide large areas of radiation. Sand is a good producer for much the same reason. Although sand color will reflect the heat more than dark colors, there are so many tiny surfaces to re-

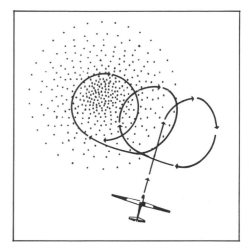

The top drawing demonstrates how a pilot centers in a thermal. As he turns, his variometer will indicate the amount of lift. He will keep shifting the position of his plane until the vario reads a consistent high value all the way around the circle. Below is a typical path a sailplane might take in order to find the lift. The pilot knows the lift is around, and searching in circles will locate it. Then it's centered.

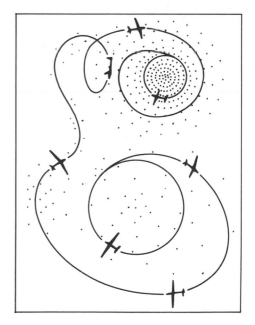

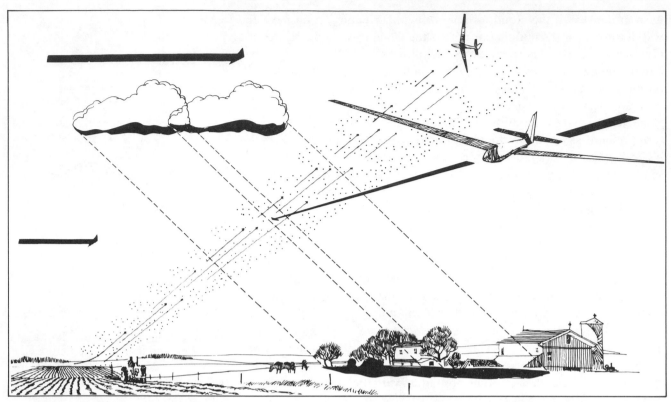

A sailplane pilot learns to "read" the land-scape. He'll know where to look for thermals and where to catch them. In this case it's a plowed field. Thermals will blow on the wind, so he'll determine wind direction by watching the cloud shadows.

ceive the sun's rays that good heating takes place. Location has to be considered. If sand sits next to a pond, it is a good bet. The air over the pond will be cool, over the sand warm and with that temperature differential, up goes the warm air.

Thick dark drops or dense wooded areas would seem to be good thermal producers, but instead they intercept much of the incoming radiation before it reaches the ground. It takes a long period of time to heat the ground in a wooded area, but once heated, the foliage acts much like a blanket. Late in the day when open fields are beginning to cool down, the wooded areas will still be warm and may very well produce thermals.

Bare ground and short crops are thermal starters. Ridges that face the sun are very good. Rock outcroppings will produce. Towns are good because they have some internal heating; fires, dumps and smokestacks can keep the thermals popping off. Asphalt parking lots and shopping centers give off good heat. Don't fly downwind of a town; the smoke and haze can form an umbrella and cut the sun off from the ground.

Finding the thermal is a matter of putting all the factors into your "computer" and getting the answer. Experience is the best and only teacher. This is something your instructor can't tell you, but you can learn a lot by flying with other pilots from your field.

Flying thermals may sound very complicated and unsafe. It's not, because you will fly and learn all of this within a five-mile radius of your airport. If you get into trouble and can't find a thermal you'll glide to the airport and land.

The Lee Wave

The lee wave or mountain wave is the most spectacular source of updraft that Mother Nature offers. The altitude record, flying the wave, is an astonishing forty-six thousand feet. That's higher than commercial jets can fly. Oxygen was the only life-support system on these flights, but with a pressure suit or cabin, that record will be broken.

What is the wave? Air is a fluid, as is water. If we think of ourselves as living at the bottom of an ocean of air, just as a fish lives at the bottom of a stream, we can explain the wave by observing what we think the fish would see. Sit on the side of the stream and take note. The water comes flowing down the stream. There is a submerged rock right in the center of the stream. The water flows against it, builds up pressure and flows over the rock, making a wave in the surface of the water. The water then dips down on the back side of the rock and an interesting thing happens. A wave is formed a foot or so downstream of the rock and another one is formed a foot or so downstream of that wave. You would think that if the first wave on the surface were formed by the rock, there must be rocks behind it forming the second and third wave . . . but there are none, as any fish can tell you. He sits behind that rock and gets his food, as will be explained soon. The water was set into the wave motion by the first rock and the speed of the water deter-

The Lee Wave's air flow has been measured as high as 100,000 feet.

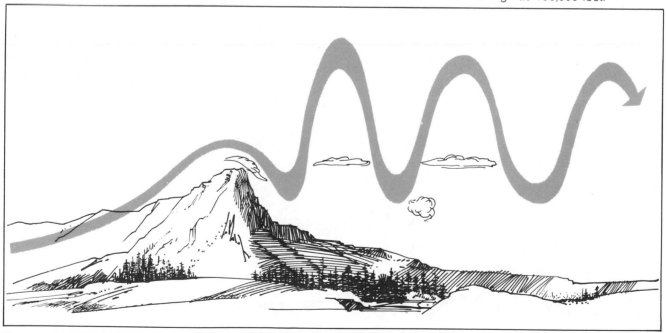

mined the size and distance between the waves that followed. The same thing happens in the air.

If we have a steady flow of air (like the stream) striking a mountain broadside (like the rock in the stream), the air will be forced over the mountain. If you could sit above it all and see it, it would look just like the wave of water going over the rock. Then downstream, in the airflow, the same phenomenon that happened in the water happens in the air. Waves are formed. If the temperature and condition of the layers of air above the mountain are right, the wave action of the air will be formed many thousands of feet higher than the mountain.

What is a wave? Float a straw down the stream and you will observe that when it hits the wave it floats up the front side, goes over the top and then down the back side. Consider now this same wave in the air. Instead of a straw, place a sailplane in this current. Put the sailplane just behind the rock (mountain), in the lowest part of the trough of the wave. As the air goes up to form the wave it'll carry the plane up, just as the water carried the straw. The trick is to stay on the up side of the wave because the flow of air on the down side is just as strong and will carry the plane down as fast as it went up.

Interestingly, the flow of air going through this wave motion is so smooth that once the sailplane is positioned correctly in the up-flow, the pilot is as steady in his cockpit as if he were sitting in an easy chair in his living room. It's not uncommon to climb a thousand feet a minute for twenty or thirty minutes on this air that's as smooth as silk. The variometer shows you the position of strongest lift. The way to fly this is to find the strongest band of lift by moving forward or backward, within the confines of the up side of the wave. You do this by increasing or decreasing the air speed of the plane. When you get the maximum lift on the variometer you hold that air speed. Then you look to the ground and find a mark, such as a road crossing. You note where it

Air and water are both fluids. The fish's-eye view of the wave is much the same as the soaring pilot's view in air.

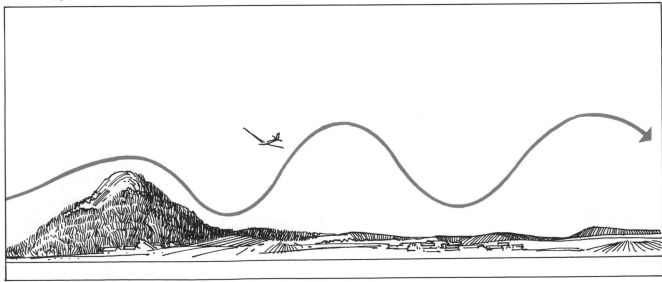

is on the canopy of your ship. You fly the ship so that your air speed is the same as the speed of the wind. You, in fact, stand still in the air with no forward or back drift motion. The only motion you have is straight up . . . on the silk.

The Rotor   Why does the fish sit behind the rock with his knife and fork ready? As the water goes over the rock and starts forming its wave motion, the fish's dinner fails to make the turns in the trough of the wave, so it falls out of the water flow . . . gobble, gobble. It's not only the fish food that can't make the turns in the wave flow—some of the water can't get around into the upswing of the wave. The water that can't get around the curves spins off with such force that it digs a hole behind the rock. The same thing happens in the air. The air that is on the fringe of the main wave motion comes down on the back side of the wave, can't make the turn and spins off, making a violent rotor that has been known to be strong enough to tear small planes apart in flight.

If there is moisture in the airflow that is traveling through the wave, a rotor cloud will pinpoint this area of violence. The cloud looks like a cotton ball, but if you study it you will see that it appears as if a boxer is inside trying to fight his way out. Sailplane pilots avoid the rotor at all costs. If there is no cloud to show where it is, the pilot, on encountering strong turbulence, will turn away and fly around the area.

How do you go down out of the wave? Slow your air speed and drift to the back side of the wave and go down, or fly ahead of it and go down out in front of it. When I flew out of a wave over Mt. Washington, New Hampshire, I left at twenty-five thousand feet, flew above the cloud system below me, all the way to the Atlantic Ocean, and still had enough altitude to turn around and fly back to the base of the mountain, under the whole system, and land.

Riding a sailplane on the up side of the wave is like floating on silk. Flying an airplane perpendicularly through the wave can spell disaster. Pilots have likened it to smashing into a brick wall.

LANDING A SAILPLANE

The Sea Breeze

The pilot who lives close to a coastline has an added form of convection. The sea breeze is formed by temperature differential. During the day, the temperature of the air over the water is cooler than the temperature of the air over the land. When the general wind velocity is low, a local wind condition is produced. As the sun heats the land mass, the air above it is warmed and rises. The constant cool air over the water rushes in to take the place of the rising air. An onshore or sea breeze is created. A narrow "wall" of convection is formed. As the air goes up and condenses it forms clouds that show the flight path.

Long flights can be made riding this "wall" in the sky, but it takes a lot of experience to find it. If the air that rises is dry, no clouds will be formed to show the way. That condition is similar to flying dry thermals. The only way to find the lift is with the variometer. The sea breeze can form over the beach or as far as fifty miles inland. If the offshore winds are light, the sea breeze will penetrate further and further inland as the day wears on. Pilots flying the breeze say, "There is a little bit of magic to it."

Landing a sailplane is safer than landing a power plane because if a problem arises there is no power to drive the plane into the ground and no fuel to burn. Sailplanes land at a slow speed. Even the high-performance ships, capable of cruising speeds of 120 miles per hour, can be landed, with flaps, at about 40 miles per hour.

Sailplanes land in the same manner as power planes. A rectangular pattern is flown over the chosen landing spot. The final touchdown is made into the wind. Because of the slow landing speeds a sailplane's rollout is short. An area the size of a football field is more than sufficient space for a landing.

Landing on an airport runway is easy to understand. The question that most people have is how does the sailplane land when it can't reach an airport? Isn't it dangerous? What happens if all of a sudden there is no more lift and the pilot has to land?

Off-field landings are not dangerous. Every soaring pilot learns the problems and how to execute the "emergency" farmer's-field landing. Instructors put students through all kinds of practice situations that simulate the kind of problems he will encounter to impress upon the student that a sailplane, unlike an airplane, cannot fly around again if the landing approach is not correct. A sailplane is committed to landing once it's below a thousand feet. It has to be brought down right. There is no second chance. Each landing at the home field is done as if it's practice for a farm-field landing. With a hundred such tries, an off-field landing will be a piece of cake. I firmly believe that most soaring pilots know more about landing than power pilots.

There is another question that bothers most people. What happens if all of a sudden the pilot runs out of lift and there are no landing places? The answer is simple. That situation is never allowed to happen. Here is why. First, things do not happen as fast as all that. Let's assume the sailplane is at two thousand feet and there is no more lift around and it must land. Depending on the weather and the kind of plane, it'll take fifteen to thirty minutes for the plane to descend to the ground from two thousand feet. That's plenty of time, and the plane can cover a distance in any direction of from five to ten miles from that altitude before the landing pattern must be started. Now, here is the rule: Although you have the ability to go five or more miles when at two thousand feet, you never leave a potential landing area once you get down to that two thousand-foot altitude. You have one thousand feet to lose before the landing pattern must be started. The pilot can search for lift in that area. If he finds it and climbs back up to, say, thirty-five hundred, he can be off and on his way again. If not, and he uses up his thousand feet of altitude searching, he has no alternative but to land at that field. This is his guarantee to always have a field available.

Here is the way that works. Let's say on a cross-country flight the pilot had climbed to five thousand feet. A half hour later he's traveled forty miles and is down to twenty-five hundred feet. It's late in the day and he realizes that there is little or no lift around. In the last three miles flown, he notes that there were four farmer's fields that looked as though they were possible landing sites. Ahead on course it looks like miles of woods. He can't see any landing areas ahead. The two thousand-foot rule is put into effect. The pilot flies on searching for lift. He can afford to lose five hundred feet in his search. Then he'll have to turn back to the fields he's seen. Let's assume that he flies on and finds no lift or any more landing areas. Back he turns, searching for lift on the way. At nineteen hundred feet he sees that the first field on his return does not look very good. The approach is lined with trees and there is heavy green foliage across the middle of the field that could mean a single-strand, barbed-wire fence. On he goes to the next field, searching for lift on the way. This one looks better, longer, no fences and can be used, but a large part of it is very dark. It looks as though the soil could be soggy. He notes the ground wind direction from some smoke. If need be, a safe landing to the north could be made in that field to miss the soggy area, but he has enough altitude to look at another field a quarter of a mile away. At fifteen hundred feet he is over the third field and sees that it's perfect. It's a hayfield and the wagon marks in the field indicate that it was cut only a few days ago. He circles the field and goes over a check list . . . no rocks . . . it's relatively flat . . . plenty long enough . . . fences only at each end . . . no telephone poles at the end he will approach. The smoke he saw at the last sight indicated a slight cross-wind landing. The trees across the road could cause some turbulence near the ground, so he plans to add five miles per hour to his landing pattern speed. With that settled he goes back to his searching for lift. He stays close to that field while searching. He keeps looking at the field, each time he turns in his search for lift, to see if there is anything about the field he missed. When he is down to a thousand feet he flies to the planned position to start the descent for landing.

The accepted landing pattern for both small power planes and sailplanes.

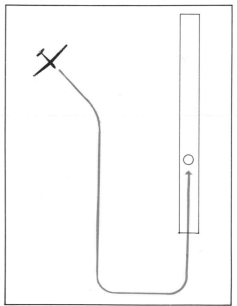

There are four legs to fly in an off-field landing. The cross-wind leg, started at a thousand feet, gives the pilot a good look at the field. He's low enough now to make out small details and he can pick the exact spot for touchdown. The pattern speed is set up and the added five miles per hour is included. The dive brakes or flaps are cracked open and tested. The descent is started. At nine hundred feet the plane is to start the downwind leg of the pattern. This leg goes fast because the wind is blowing from behind the plane. The dive brakes are extended so that at the end of this leg the ship will be down to six hundred feet above the ground. The base leg is across the wind and sets the plane up for the final glide to touchdown. Adjustments in direction and altitude are made. The final leg is what the pattern is all about. With his eye on the touchdown spot, the pilot can still make corrections by adding more or less dive brake. He can land long or short of his point if he sees an obstacle at the last minute. Once the decision is finally made, he makes his angle of descent, shifts his eyes to the far end of the field and flies the plane down. A few feet off the ground he pulls the stick back slightly and allows the plane to fly parallel to the ground. The air speed will slow down as the plane flies on the ground cushion of air and touches down. The wheel brake is applied instantly . . . dive brakes applied full out and the plane stops only after a short rollout . . . one wing settles to the ground.

That description should dispel the notion that suddenly while gliding around in the air you have to land . . . as if it's all a big panic. It's not. It took half an hour, at least, from twenty-five hundred feet, when the woods loomed ahead and the flight couldn't go on because of the two thousand-foot rule, to touchdown. That's the planning every soaring pilot learns.

The sequence of pictures was the result of a poorly planned and executed landing pattern. He skimmed in just over the trees, and his last-minute turn was too late. The wing tip actually touched the ground, as its shadow indicates. If one observes the 1,000-foot rule, this could never happen, but, as in this case, sometimes competition pilots push their luck. This pilot, who is a very experienced competitor, would have had to land in a field a mile from the airport if he had made a full-pattern landing. The competition director chewed him out, saying it was better to be safe than to win.

The sailplane is the most graceful of all the flying machines. It can outfly the birds in every way. This sequence of pictures on the next eight pages will enable you to see and feel your way around the loop. This maneuver was started at 4,000 feet. The nose was put down, the speed increased, and a dive was started. At 3,000 feet, the air speed reached 120 mph, then the control stick was slowly started back. The first picture was taken when rotation out of the dive started. Hold your breath and turn the page. . . .

Air speed is traded off for altitude. We'll regain the 1,000 feet we lost in the dive and, if not careful, some of our breakfast. The centrifugal force pushes you into your seat on the way up, but at the top you feel weightless. The world goes under you and, if you can find your breath, you want to scream for the joy of it all. Take a breath as stick is pulled back in your lap and turn the page . . . .

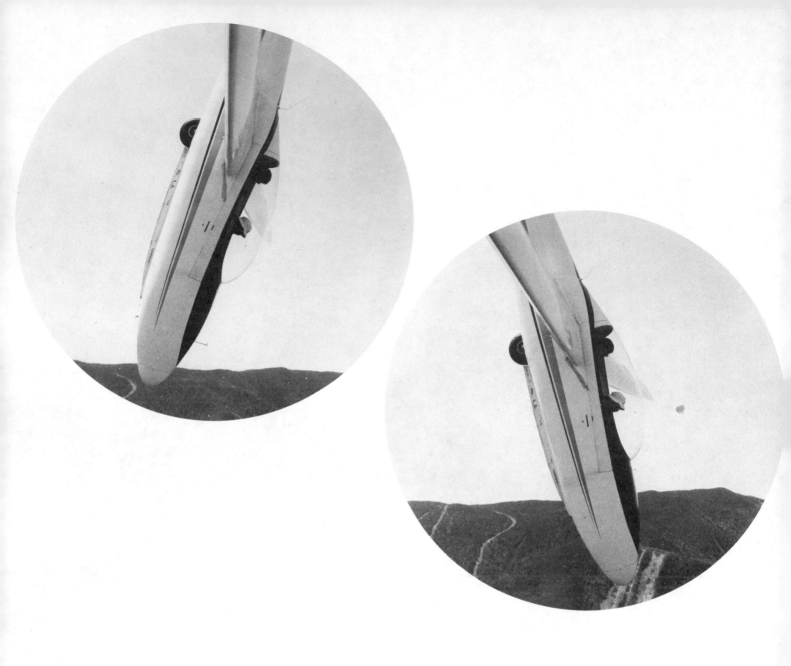

Over the top and into the last part of the loop is when the "G" loading builds up. The wind sings a fun song; you laugh out of excitement; your muscles tense up and your blood doesn't know which way to flow.

These pictures were taken by mounting a Nikon F2 camera with motor drive on a strut that protruded two feet ahead of the wing. The camera was set to take two pictures a second. A 20mm lens was used. The camera was fired electrically by running a wire back to the cockpit. The author, who was flying the plane, also took the pictures. The complete sequence consisted of 24 pictures.

SOARING ... A STEP-BY-STEP SPORT

The first ride as a passenger in a sailplane is a rather overwhelming experience. The neophyte has enough trust that he'll take the ride; if he likes it (and most do), the next question is "Could I do it?" For those without any experience in the air it looks complicated. With a little knowledge and experience you'll see the way. Going to the moon looks scary, too. Guys like Neil Armstrong (who, incidentally, flies sailplanes) didn't just fly off to the moon. Their training was extensive. Learning to fly and then becoming an experienced soaring pilot are gradual, step-by-step processes.

I didn't get interested in soaring until I was forty-eight years old. The only thing I'd flown before that was into a rage now and then. When I stepped out of the trainer after my demonstration flight, my knees were shaking and I was giddy, but I liked it. A week later, when I took my first lesson, the knees were okay ... step one. Then my instructor took me through the training ... step two. During those first lessons, I remember thinking about what I wanted to do with this new skill, if I could actually learn to fly one of these machines. I felt that there was no use to go on for a license; just soloing would be enough satisfaction. Step three: After solo, I figured I might as well take the license because I saw people flying for hours on the ridge that ran alongside the airport. That seemed like fun, so I rented a plane and joined them. With pencil and paper in hand, I figured that the rental of the plane, costing ten dollars an hour, was going to add up to a lot of money, so I bought myself a plane. It wasn't till later when my bank account was getting low that I discovered my error. I'd forgotten to figure in the cost of the fur coat. After all, it was only the right and decent thing to buy my wife a coat if I was going to buy myself a plane.

I was hooked, because every step along the way gave such a sense of satisfaction and personal accomplishment. Solo was the first breakthrough; it was like getting permission from mother to go to the park by myself and play with the other kids. I'd wake up in the middle of the night chuckling to myself ... "I flew all by myself!" It didn't make any difference to me that my time in the air was about the same as Wilbur Wright's record set sixty-five years earlier or that the same day that I soloed astronauts were circling the moon. They couldn't have been any more excited than I was.

It wasn't the four thousand for the plane that committed me to the sport; it was the plane. If it rained on the weekend I went to the airport anyway just to pat her. Even though she was an old lady, I loved her. We flew that ridge for hours at a time to land only when my bladder screamed from neglect. Up and back we glided until we knew every tree on the way. We scared hell out of the birds in the spring ... they got used to us by summer ... bored with us by fall and flew away. We were there to see the snow fill the empty nests. When the birds returned in the spring I was ready to leave ... almost.

The very idea of flying off into the wild blue yonder and going cross-country without an instructor in the back seat to pull me out of a jam was not comforting. I was ready to go, but couldn't. Knowing very well that I could land my plane anywhere was no help. There was always some excuse for not leaving "mother," but I wanted to go so badly that I dreamed about it. Dreams became nightmares. At three A.M., every night for weeks, I'd bolt upright in bed and holler out loud, "You got to be out of your cotton-pickin' mind." The dream was always the same. I'd be flying at three thousand feet over the airport, reach for the radio and announce to my crew below, "I'm off. I'm going cross-country." In my dream I was also the crew on the ground working the radio in my car, and I was shouting my "honest" opinion back to me.

Every pilot goes through the agony of this ambivalence. Finally, with a hundred local flights under my belt, with a well-planned flight to an airport thirty-two miles away, and a ground crew primed for any emergency, I was off. Thirty-two miles later, with no airport in sight, down to two thousand feet with no more lift around, I knew the flight was over. Taking no chances, and with a good pasture below, I wasn't about to fly off seeking more lift. Circling around that field, losing altitude slowly, I knew every detail about it, including the fact that the

THE BIG STEP . . . THE OFF-FIELD LANDING

Off-field landings are never done except in cross-country flying. It is not dangerous and a common occurrence in competition flying. Sailplane landings are relatively safe because speeds are not as fast as in power flying, but more importantly, if something does go wrong, there is no power to drive you into the ground or fuel to burn.

farmer had a daughter. The female dainties on the clothesline, which also showed the wind direction, announced that fact. My circling bird drew the attention of the farmer and his daughter; they were out watching me. At a thousand feet I settled down to the big job . . . to land the bloody machine. It was a perfect landing! Almost before I stopped, the farmer and his daughter were driving their truck out into the field to welcome me. Too excited to talk, all I could do was sit there and giggle . . . pleased with myself. As I unstrapped my parachute, still sitting in the cockpit, I was amazed to see their expressions change from sheer delight to expressions of horror. The daughter put her hands over her mouth, out of fear. Both stood gazing, wide-eyed. I followed their gazes down to my white shirt . . . there was a bright red stain as big as a fist covering my heart. "My God," I thought, "after such a perfect landing, I'm going to die!" A red felt pen in my pocket had leaked.

I had a few more surprises. Asking the farmer where I was, he gave me the name of the town. That wasn't enough information for me—I didn't even know what county or state I was in. Finding the spot on my chart, I realized that on this very first cross-country flight a possible world record had been made. I did my thirty-two miles, but I was fifty miles off course, and that *had* to be some sort of a record.

NAVIGATING CROSS-COUNTRY

Since I can get lost walking down the street, navigation needed special attention. Before that first flight I'd pored over aircraft charts, vicariously flying all kinds of missions. Drawing a line from my airport to the destination, I'd marked off a notch, on the line, every five miles on the way . . . just as the books said to do. Figuring the compass heading for the flight, I'd then studied everything on the route that would make a good visual landmark. What would it really look like from the air? Would I recognize it? . . . obviously I didn't, but that flight did something great. Every pilot goes through indecision about going cross-country. Before they go they think, "If God wanted us to fly, he'd have given us wings." After they go the first time they think, "If God wanted us to stay on the ground, he'd have given us roots."

Cross-country flights are made up of a series of climbs to altitude in thermals and long glides between them.

A competition pilot goes over his flight plan with his ground crew. They will follow him by car with the plane's trailer hitched behind. Knowing the weather conditions, the pilot can come close in planning where he will be and at what time he will arrive.

Actually, navigating a sailplane is rather simple. Visibility is always good. You never fly in bad weather since there is no lift then. Aircraft charts show every conceivable kind of landmark and it's easy to learn the "road." It's not always possible to know exactly where you are by following a compass course and relating it to your marked route on a map. The trick is not to question the compass, as beginners want to do, but to fly on course until you recognize a landmark on the ground that you see on the chart. It always comes together before panic sets in.

One of my flying buddies, on hearing about my "world record" flight, decided to give me a lesson in navigation. As an old navy pilot he was an expert. He suggested that when I got to the top of a thermal and was on course, I look for lakes way out ahead. They were the easiest things to spot. Then he suggested that when I found another thermal and circled 'round and 'round to climb in it, instead of flying out of the thermal, like spinning off a top, I should look for my lakes. By remembering where they had been before I went into the thermal, I'd stay on course by lining them up again. I couldn't wait to get into the air and try his scheme. It didn't work . . . there weren't any lakes within a hundred miles.

Good pilot navigation is also important for the ground crew. They follow below on the roads, pulling the sailplane's trailer over hill and dale, staying as close to the sailplane as possible. During my early cross-country experiences I spent a thousand dollars to put aircraft radio in my sailplane and in the family car, only to get up and stay aloft for four hours and never use the radio once. When I finally landed I used the planned emergency telephone number. My wife was rather put out with me when we managed to get together late that night by phone. 'Why didn't you use your thousand-dollar radio and tell me where you were?" "How could I?" I answered. "I didn't know where I was." In twenty minutes she picked me up. She watched the weather and knew more about what the plane and I would do than I did. I learned a few things on that flight. One, if radio contact is lost, give a full description of what you do see and let the crew know that you are still in the air. They may be able to hear you, but they may not be able to transmit to you because of mountain ranges in the way. Two, take some navigation lessons from my wife.

For a good competition pilot, soaring can be a rather solitary sport, but not for me. The idea of the sport is to go up, spend four or eight hours aloft, alone in the cockpit, race around the course, get home and win the prizes. I found it very different. I'd get up, fly two or three hours, make a turn point eighty miles away and lose my lift and have to land. It was always a big happening wherever I landed. People came from miles to see the plane that "crashed" in Farmer Brown's hayfield. I never carried food with me on a flight. I received dinner invitations that became feasts served on the Sunday dishes. Unfortunately, of the hundreds of farmers I dropped in on, none of them had daughters over eleven years old.

I always carried liability insurance, assuming some day I'd meet up with a nasty farmer. One day it almost happened. I landed in this good field and the farmhand came running out to me and said that I'd better get that thing out of the field before the farmer came home. He in no uncertain terms told me that his boss was meaner than a bull and as stubborn as a jackass. My crew arrived; we raced to get the plane apart, into the trailer and be off. As we finished, the farmer came speeding across the field in his Cadillac. I could tell by the way he jammed on the brakes and jumped out of the car that trouble was coming. I told my crew that I'd handle this. What I didn't see was that the farmer was carrying two bottles of chilled champagne. He was so elated to see a glider up close that he even offered the farmhand a drink. He was so pleased that for the next four days, Farmer Ed Spores joined my ground crew. A Christmas hasn't passed since that we haven't received a card from that beautiful farmer . . .

FOR THOSE WHO NEVER CUT THE CORD

It's not necessary to fly cross-country to enjoy this sport. About 80 percent of pilots stay within gliding distance of the home field. This will vary according to conditions. They will spend hours aloft, chatting with each other by radio and helping one another find lift. Many fields are situated so that combinations of lift are available. On a good day a pilot can start on a ridge, find a thermal popping off a rock face that's heated by the sun, and fly it up to a wave. The days that the ridge is the only working lift, he'll stay within three miles of home. When the thermals carry him to five thousand feet, he'll feel safe ten or so miles upwind of the airport. At ten thousand feet in the wave, he'd feel comfortable sitting twenty miles away, knowing that he'd be able to get back to the airport barbecue in time.

Local flying is in the same kind of air as cross-country flying. It takes the same kind of skill to stay up and no one can say that it's not as much fun. If you are in a sport for relaxation, and change of pace from office life, local flying is a good answer.

CLUB ACTIVITY

Much of the fun of soaring is social. Although more and more women are getting into the sport, most of the pilots are men. In good weather it becomes a family activity. Practically all of the 250 gliding centers in the country have organized themselves into clubs which will take care of social needs. The range of activities they perform varies from a simple Saturday-night barbecue around a charcoal pit to having dinner in their own social hall equipped with kitchen. Although the pilot is completely on his own in the air, it's a different matter on the ground. The planes are most graceful flying; on the ground they're awkward and need a few hands. It becomes a cooperative affair. Some clubs own their own sailplanes and tow planes. Everyone chips in and does the work so it becomes a rather inexpensive way to fly. Some of the clubs are set up on fields that have a commercial operator and some are completely independent, with hangars, shops, instructors, even bunkhouses and areas for families to set up trailers or camp out. Soaring pilots will do anything necessary to sit around comfortably and tell "fish stories" about their flying experience of the day.

Many soaring families will hook the plane and trailer on the back of their cars and go off vacationing at different clubs. If the distance is too far to trail the plane they'll rent at the club of their choice. Much like the golfer, the fun is in "playing the different courses" and meeting others with the same interest.

SOARING AWARDS AND ACHIEVEMENTS

Almost every enthusiast who stays with the sport sooner or later gets involved with the personal soaring achievement awards. The awards start out on such an easy level that even the students get caught up with winning. A, B and C Badges are for solo flight, a five-minute flight and a thirty-minute flight, in that order. The Soaring Society of America gives lapel pins to those who have accomplished the simple achievements.

These early badges are a "come-on" for the more advanced awards, which also start out easy. The required tasks are set up by the Fédération Aeronautique Internationale, a worldwide body headquartered in Paris. There are three categories: Silver, Gold and Diamond "C" awards. No matter what country a pilot lives in, he must achieve the same tasks and give the required proof to his national soaring society; then he may wear the F.A.I. Badge.

SILVER . . . GOLD . . . DIAMOND

There are three tasks for each badge. For silver, the pilot must make an altitude gain of 3,281 feet (1,000 meters), a duration flight of five hours and a cross-country flight of at least thirty-one miles (50 kilometers). You can see how the new pilot can get "conned" into this game. On a good day, a climb of three thousand to four thousand feet is not too difficult. For sending a copy of his barograph tracing to the S. S. A., he'll receive a letter stating that it has recorded the first leg of his Silver Badge achievement. The letter praises him for his good work, so he prepares for the next achievement by going without water and coffee before takeoff to try to stay aloft for five hours.

The third leg, a cross-country flight of thirty-one miles, is the one that separates the men from the boys. It's not the distance, it's the thought of landing out that scares them off. When one finally gets his nerve up and wins the Silver, this leg makes it a thrilling achievement. I knew one pilot who was so proud that he wore the Silver Badge on his pajamas.

The Gold Badge is a big step. There is no doubt that the pilot who wears it has the respect of his colleagues. The first leg is a five-hour duration flight, and he may use the same flight that qualified him for the Silver. That's good psychology on the part of the F. A. I. It means that the pilot with his Silver Badge is already started on his Gold. An altitude gain of 9,843 feet (3,000 meters) is the second leg. This is the little hard to come by in many parts of the world, but the third leg is the one that takes skill. It's a cross-country flight of 187 miles (300 kilometers).

The top awards are the three Diamonds and the pilot can wear one with his Gold Badge as he achieves each task. One is for a climb of 16,404 feet (5,000 meters). Another represents a flight of 187 miles with a preannounced turn point, which is more difficult than the straight flight of the same distance for the Gold Badge. The last Diamond is for flying a distance of 310.7 miles (500 kilometers). There are parts of the world where pilots must wait years for the right conditions to make this flight.

Soaring competitions are held at small airports where there is practically no commercial traffic. Here at Sugarbush, Vermont, where a regional championship is held, the airport's business is sports flying.

Competition pilot Dr. Ken Hamilton figures out his flight plan for the day's task. The winner will be the pilot who goes around the triangle, Sugarbush, Rutland, Lebanon, and return, in the fastest time. On a good day, that flight of 120 miles can be done in three hours or less.

SOARING COMPETITION

The first Silver award was presented in Germany in 1928 to Herr Kronfeld for his ninety-mile flight in a storm. One of Hitler's first acts was to take the badge away from him and present it to an Aryan. Fifty years after the first Silver Badge was awarded there are fewer than two thousand pilots in the world who have achieved all three Diamonds. The Gold Badge with a cluster of gems is difficult to win. It is truly an accomplishment worthy of all the dreams, frustrations and anxieties pilots have had trying for it.

In soaring, just staying aloft is a contest. Once that's been mastered it's only natural to see how you do against your fellow pilots. Outclimbing another plane working the same thermal, going higher or farther is the stuff that finally leads to world records, or at the very least some fast talk around the Saturday-night barbecue at the airport.

Flight became competitive the moment it was invented. Contests were held in Europe before World War I. In 1930 the first national con-

Planes are ready for take-off. They go one at a time. The wing boy runs the wing until the tow plane has gotten up to speed. Once aloft, all the planes will be towed to a specific spot and they will drop off tow at 2,000 feet above the ground. The start gate is an imaginary window in the sky. The plane is timed as he goes through the "window." Then he flies out on course.

There is some luck, little guesswork, and a lot of skill to competition flying. SF races for home at 150 mph.

Time-keeping and scoring takes a team of workers and a computer to put on a good contest. Regionals are five-day events.

Ground crews stay in touch with their pilots by aircraft radio. The crew waits for the words "Go home".

Ken Hamilton's crew got home in time to inform him on landing that he had won the event. It's a long, tiring, exhausting day; turn the page to see how Ken took a busman's holiday to relax.

test was held in this country at Elmira, New York. Today, for those who like a challenge and have the passion to compete, soaring can provide the way.

Local soaring meets involve modest cross-country flights, such as a triangle with twenty-mile legs. They are usually weekend events and are a good way to get competition experience. The next step is the regional meets sponsored by the Soaring Society of America. To enter, a pilot must have won his Silver Badge. Regionals are five-day events and involve flights of about three hundred miles. In many ways soaring contests are like yacht races. The course is set according to the weather conditions and the winner is the one who completes the course in the shortest time. A Gold Badge, plus achieving standing in a regional meet, is one way to qualify for the National Soaring Championships, a ten-day event, in which a champion is named. From the National Championships, a team is picked to represent the country in the World Competition, which is held every two years. Normally twenty-five to thirty countries participate with as many as one hundred planes divided into classes according to their performance. Competition planes cost anywhere from fourteen thousand to twenty-five thousand and are aerodynamically the cleanest planes that fly.

All the active sports make a man restless. The mountain climber wants to conquer every peak. The golfer has to play the most famous courses around the world. The sailor dreams about skippering a sloop into Captain Kidd's Cove, and the balloonist's craving is to cross the spectacular Swiss Alps. The soaring pilot is no different. Once I had seen the Alps from a balloon, I knew I had to fly that country in a glider.

Once our crew crossed into Italy, the spectacle below changed. The rugged snow-capped peaks gave way to forests dressed in every hue of green imaginable. From eleven thousand feet Lake Como and Lago Maggiore sparkled like sapphires. As if the Alps themselves weren't enough, this was all an unexpected added treat. While silently standing in a wicker basket drinking it all in, suddenly something white and moving caught my eye. I could hardly believe what I was seeing. There, eight thousand feet below, were the four sailplanes I mentioned in "Swiss Balloonacy," flying in formation wingtip to wingtip. The scene below initiated a whole new idea. Why not fly a glider in the dramatic setting of the Swiss Alps? Why not soar around the Matterhorn! I spent a restless year until the idea became a reality.

In August, a year later, I was met at the Zurich airport by Adrian Marx, a Swiss soaring pilot. We sat at the bar and he filled me in on our final plans. We were to fly a two-seater motor glider from a little airport at Hausen, a half-hour drive outside of Zurich. Adrian must have seen the frown on my face as he mentioned the motor glider, so he went on to explain. "We've got to travel ninety miles to get to Visp, a town on the Rhone at the foot of the Alps. Once we get there we'll turn the motor off; it's not going to do us any good, anyway, once we're about nine thousand feet. We'll have to soar to climb the rest of the way up."

A ONCE-IN-A-LIFETIME FLIGHT

As much as I hate motors, all kinds—outboards, inboards, lawn-mowers, snowmobiles and even cars—I accepted what Adrian said. The rest of his story convinced me that the idea of a motor wasn't too bad. The country we might have to fly over was rough and desolate and the thing that concerned him most was a storm that was moving up through Italy. With luck, good weather would hold for twenty-four hours. Once the bad weather moved in, he expected it to be around for about four days. I'd scheduled only three days for this flight. It was now or never. I was going to try to talk him into using a two-seater sailplane until he mentioned the weather problem . . . hate 'em or not, that motor might come in handy.

We were at the airport at seven the next morning. A weather check indicated that if we kept our fingers crossed we might make it. With lunch, cameras and charts aboard, we taxied out to the runway. The little sixty-horsepower modified VW engine had us airborne in no time flat. No 747, it, but we did manage to clear the trees at the end of the runway. As the crow flies, our flight would be about a hundred miles to the Matterhorn. We figured over two hours each way for two reasons. First, this plane does not fly as fast as a crow and, second, we'd have to follow the valleys.

Swiss countryside from a slow, low-flying plane is like a child's dream of strange lands . . . a dollhouse setting, brilliant in color. Bright chalets dotted the landscape. Villages were a cluster of neat houses. Any minute a child's hand could have reached down into the setting to move a cow to another pasture or to push the train that runs next to the azure blue river. It seemed unreal. The putt-putt of our little engine was just as unreal. Adrian pointed out landmarks—Zug Sea . . . Luzern—he was following a chain of lakes. As we progressed south, the mountains started to peek at us through the slight blue haze. Were those snowcaps in the distance? I could feel my heart pound in VW time. We turned southwest to follow the Aare River. The walls of the valley seemed to reach up and turn into passes. We moved in against walls of the pass to take advantage of the ridge lift. At the Grimsel pass we saw the Rhone River . . . gorgeous wine country. We followed it down to Visp. The Rhone is in a valley whose walls go up to form mountains, but at Visp the river meets a pass that made my mouth drop open. Visible through that pass was the largest collection of mountains in all of Europe. Twenty spectacular miles up that pass was Zermatt. Now we were at an altitude where the air was getting so thin that our little engine would be of no value to us; the switch was turned off. As far as climbing was concerned, if we wanted to get to the snowcapped fourteen thousand-footers ahead we'd have to soar for them.

It was clear from our charts and maps that there was only one way to reach the Matterhorn. Picture a bowl at the top of Switzerland whose wall is ten thousand feet high. In a ring around the bowl stand twenty-seven of Europe's thirty-seven mountains that are over four thousand meters (thirteen thousand feet). At the bottom of this spectacular setting, nestled at the base of the bowl, sits Zermatt. The north side of the bowl has a "flaw" that becomes the entranceway into the bowl. This pass starts at Visp, altitude twenty-one hundred feet, and winds its way twenty miles up into the bowl to Zermatt, altitude fifty-one hundred feet. So, there are only two ways to the "top of the world." Either you climb over the ten thousand-foot rim at some point or you go up the pass. Skiers and climbers get there by a breathtaking cog railway trip from Visp. We planned to fly, climb into the bowl on the ridge lift. Our plan was to use the prevailing wind and ridge-soar the mountains that made up the pass. When we got up into the bowl we'd fly the ridge lift, gaining altitude at each mountain in turn around the perimeter of the bowl. The mountains fit our plan exactly; each could be used like a step. Halfway around the bowl we'd be at the Monta Rosa, the highest peak of them all. Here we expected to gain enough altitude to make a beeline glide to the Matterhorn. Our retreat was the same plan, reversed . . . around the bowl and a straight glide down the pass to Visp. The maps and charts confirmed my suspicion . . . there was no place to land in the bowl except possibly on a glacier.

We pointed the nose of the little glider up the pass toward the entrance to this land of the giants. There stood the Distelhorn, a mere baby mountain of only nine thousand feet. With the motor off, Adrian turned the controls over to me. I moved in close to its southwest wall and we felt the ridge lift on the seat of our pants as the variometer registered a steady, hard up! . . . Up! We took advantage of every climbing inch and headed our little glider to the first of the snowtopped mountains . . . the Dom. We slid over close to find the face that produced the lift. I turned the controls back to Adrian so I could drink in the scenery; it was mind-boggling. The beauty of snow and rock was stupendous. I spied four climbers roped together plodding their way up what looked like an impossible spine of ice. It was an unreal world.

It should be said here that no camera can capture the real Zermatt and its surrounding spectacle. If pictures cannot express the vastness of this region, its beauty, its emotional impact on an individual, I humbly and categorically state that my words can in no way measure up to this impossible task. If God wanted man to see His spectacular creation from a vantage point, He would have had man invent a sailplane, so he could glide quietly among His works of beauty and terror that He built side by side.

At four thousand meters, the mountain climber's magic number because anything above it is considered a major climb, we silently glided to the top of the Taschhorn, and against its rock face we circled and picked up enough altitude to fly to the next peak, where I had my first real look at a glacier. It was awesome. The Monta Rosa sits between two glaciers. We nestled into its western face to gain altitude and there the climbers waved their ice axes in greeting.

Back and forth we wove a path in front of the face. With each pass we gained hundreds of feet. When we first saw the climbers they were above us. In only minutes we were looking down on them. We could see them stop and marvel at our ascent, and I'm sure they wished they had wings. As we made our last pass we waved to them. The leader grabbed the ice ax of the second person in line and held the two axes at

The author and Swiss pilot Adrian Marx prepare to leave for their 90-mile flight from the Zurich area to the Alps. Once they reached 9,000 feet, they turned off their engine and soared, using the mountain currents. The engine was of no value above that altitude. The soaring was spectacular and the Swiss scenery breathtaking.

arm's length and flapped them. We waggled our wings in salute. We flew on to the Breithorn; I photographed the climbers sunning themselves on its snowcapped peak. The sunlight was dazzling so high in this world.

The Breithorn is separated from the Matterhorn only by the width of the Theodul Glacier . . . maybe five miles wide. How long does it take to glide five miles? In that short time, from absolute blue sky to the time we reached the king of all mountains in Europe, the weather changed and a shawl of clouds moved up from Italy to partially engulf the majestic mountain. These sudden weather changes are a great fear of the alpine climber . . . and I must say the alpine glider pilot, too. We raced against the approaching weather that was brewing itself from sunbeams. We had hoped to circle the Matterhorn and photograph it from all sides; clouds already blocked the Italian face and the west wall.

The lift was strong and we maneuvered in close to see the treacherous north face, which has claimed hundreds of lives since the mountain was first conquered. How anyone could climb that sheer wall was beyond my comprehension. It was frightening to be near. I banked the glider over hard and turned away; below, the scene was just as awesome. The glacier, in the shadow of the rock that stands as no other rock in the world, was gray, death white. No wonder this was the last mountain of Europe to be conquered. The glacier's gnarled surface hinted at its own age. Within its bowels it still holds the Reverend Hudson, who dared to conquer the Matterhorn with Edward Whymper in 1865, only to fall after that first triumphal ascent. Turning away, I felt more comfortable at a safe distance, where the mountain had a majestic look; up close it was fearsome. It's the only mountain, of the hundreds

Every soaring flight seems to have its own excitement. Altitude flights on the wave are memorable; distance flights cross-country are a challenge. This flight past the summit of the Matterhorn, a once-in-a-lifetime experience, has to have been my wildest and most beautiful flight. The picture was shot remotely by the author, using a motor-drive Nikon on the wing tip and a 20mm lens.

around the bowl, that is not covered with snow year round. It's too steep; it sheds its snow. A monument of rock, detached, thrust up to remind all of "the omnipotent strength."

Adrian and I were so infatuated by the vista and our own private thoughts that we forgot about the weather. I was jerked out of my private world by his saying, "Hey, let's get out of here."

In those few minutes, the weather had moved in so fast that the sunny Breithorn was now murky in shadow and the Liskamm and Monta Rosa were almost gone. The way back around the bowl to Visp would be blocked in minutes. Our only escape now was over the ten thousand-foot west rim, toward the clear sky in the d'Heren Valley.

We dared not go below ten thousand feet or our little motor might not get us to safety over the rim at Dent Blanche. Adrian turned in his seat, as far as his safety straps would allow; I could see the smile on his face as he pointed above us. There a cumulus cloud was being formed over the Zmutt Glacier. Its first wisps were building fast. He turned our little engine on; the putt, putt, putt was a comforting sound. Our altimeter was reading eleven thousand, four hundred feet. It's possible we could have reached the rim without the motor, but with that thermal in sight, we were golden. I banked the little glider over sharply as the wingtip bumped up, announcing the rising air. We circled and climbed for only a few minutes and had two thousand feet in the bag. We headed for the rim.

As we cleared the last rock wall, by about three hundred feet, I banked the plane and started a 360-degree turn. I wanted one last look. For a moment I thought I'd lost my bearing as I turned. The mountains had vanished! They were all gone, as if they had never existed. I laughed and said to Adrian, "I expect any second to wake up and find myself sitting bolt upright in bed, wide-eyed, peering into the darkness of the bedroom searching for my dream." I couldn't hear his answer; the rain was pelting our canopy.

The three-hour flight back to Hausen was uneventful according to Adrian, but my story is different. These alpine pilots are a breed unto themselves. With Visp blocked, we went across the Gimmi Pass. We managed to stay on the edge of the storm but the Gimmi was the most treacherous country I ever flew over. Landing anywhere in this twenty-mile stretch was an impossibility.

It was a relief to get out of the mountain area. Not that I was afraid that we would fly into a storm, but instead that the storm would fly into us. I've seen weather make its change instantly in this kind of country. Storm clouds do not necessarily move in . . . this is where they form. A change in temperature occurs, and instantly you are engulfed.

With thirty miles to go and plenty of altitude, we glided the rest of the way home to Hausen to beat the storm.

We rolled the plane into the hangar . . . and got soaked doing it. For four days the Monta Rosa, the Breithorn, the Matterhorn and all their sisters hid their heads.

And so ended a magnificent experience . . . maybe a once-in-a-lifetime . . . or a one of a kind.

The Federal Aviation Administration regulates all soaring activities in the United States. Actually it's done with the cooperation of the Soaring Society of America. If you want to get started in this sport and you have no personal contacts to direct you, it can all be done through the Soaring Society. There are about fourteen thousand dues-paying members and there is soaring activity in every state. You can learn to soar at a commercially operated school. To solo and get a private pilot's license with glider rating will cost between $550 and $750. You can join a club and take your training for less money. You will be working and learning as part of the operation. No medical examination is necessary and the minimum age for becoming licensed is sixteen, but a student may solo at age fourteen. There is no upper age limit in soaring.

Yearly dues to the Soaring Society are twenty dollars. The Society has many benefits for its members. They do oversee all of the soaring operations in the country and their safety record is very good. The student training program is well organized, comprehensive and strictly follows the regulations set down by the FAA. A student license is necessary. It is obtained from your instructor, and it's free. You can fly on a student license for twenty-four months, then it must be renewed. You may fly solo with the student license, but you cannot carry passengers. To get the license, a student will need thirty aero tows and ten hours of flying time. The student must take a written examination given by the FAA. If he passes the written test and demonstrates satisfactorily to his instructor that he will make a qualified pilot, he will be signed out for a flight test with an FAA examiner. It'll take about three months of weekend flying at a commercial school to get a license. Some schools will give concentrated courses that will produce a license in ten days to two weeks.

Sailplanes have become extremely sophisticated flying machines. Few are built from kits these days. The price is directly proportional to the L/D. The higher the glide ratio, the more expensive. A low-performance ship will cost about seven thousand dollars and a high one will be close to twenty thousand dollars. There are two-seaters and single-seaters in the high- and low-performance ranges. You don't necessarily have to fly a high-performance plane to have fun. The Schweizer 1-26 is a low-performance ship, but there are so many of them in this country that they have their own class competitions. A sailplane is an excellent investment because there is a big secondhand market and the value does not drop. As the prices of new planes go up the prices of used ones follow.

There are three kinds of competition in soaring. The first is against yourself. You can try to accomplish a set of tasks set down by the international FAI. The Soaring Society oversees all the record attempts. You can win badges with different ratings. The tests start out easy, but it'll take real proficiency to do such things as fly cross-country 311 miles or free climb sixteen thousand feet. The second kind of competition is against your fellow pilots. This is a series of tasks around a course against time. Every two years a world championship is held. The third type of competition is in world records. The important ones are distance and speed. Flights of over 1,000 miles have now been made.

Soaring magazine is a must for anyone interested in this sport. Write to The Soaring Society of America, P.O. Box 66071, Los Angeles, California 90066. A subscription is included with the S. S. A. membership dues of twenty dollars. You will also receive a Soaring Directory which lists every member by state and lists clubs, schools and just about any conceivable fact associated with the sport, its past, present and future.

Books on soaring could almost fill a library. Some are good and some are superficial in their coverage. For the beginner and student pilot, *The Art and Technique of Soaring* by R. A. Wolters, McGraw-Hill, is a solid book covering all phases of the sport. It's a training manual, illustrated heavily with motor-drive sequence pictures used as a learning tool. For the true enthusiast, competitor and pro, *Winning on the Wind* by World Champion George Moffat is an excellent book published by Aviation Book Co.

The big mail-order houses in the sport are Rainco, P.O. Box 20944, Phoenix, Arizona 85036, and Graham Thomson Ltd., 3200 Airport Ave., Santa Monica, California 90405. Both companies can supply you with everything from a high-performance European-made sailplane to the clothes to wear when flying. The biggest American manufacturer of sailplanes is the Schweizer Aircraft Corp., 1 Airport Road, Elmira, New York 14902. This company has been responsible for the promotion of the sport in the United States. The school they run at Elmira is the best in the country.

4
HANG GLIDING
FLYING BY THE SEAT OF YOUR PANTS

$\mathbf{H}$ang gliding, sky surfing or whatever you want to call it is the fastest-growing sport in the world of flight. To date, in the short history of aviation, this is truly the closest man has come to emulating the soaring birds.

Aviation made a hop, skip and a jump once the Wright brothers appeared on the scene . . . from Kitty Hawk to the moon in less than seventy years. Once power was applied to the wing, speed became the obsession of man in the air. Soaring and ballooning were left to the few diehards, traditionalists, sportsmen (to be kinder), who were considered as some sort of nuts as powered flight made giant steps. But the greatest technical achievement, the moon landing, brought an even bigger giant step—backward. The NASA program refined the invention of Francis Rogallo, which solved the problems that had killed Otto Lilienthal. Low, slow flight, put on the shelf for almost three-quarters of a century, was reborn.

Hang gliding is a direct outgrowth of a one-dollar kid's kite. Francis Rogallo and his wife, Gertrude, applied for a patent on what they called a "Flexible Kite" in 1948. It was a nonrigid construction, using no sticks or rigid framework. It was soon discovered that if a load is attached to the bridles instead of a string, the kite is converted to a glider. The glider could be scaled upward to carry cargo loads or people. NASA took a serious look at the Rogallo designs as a possible reentry glider for space capsules. Leonardo da Vinci had given serious consideration to the flexible wing concept. The hang glider is just such a wing with ridged supports that do not interfere with its nonridged form.

Actually, the sport of hang gliding had its real start in the nineteenth century. It took a "time out" for over half a century. Otto Lilienthal

Otto Lilienthal, the inspiration for the Wright brothers and the father of flying for the soaring pilots, stands ready to take off. Actually the hang glider pilots now claim him as one of their own . . . and they are right!

gets credit for being the first hang glider pilot. His flights in the early 1890s with a wing modeled in the configuration and structure of the stork's proved that flying was practical. His wing was in many respects similar to the basic Rogallo. Wing area, weight, structure and performance were about the same. It's interesting that many of the problems that he tried to solve are the same ones that today's pilots are working on.

Here is an account by an American journalist who visited Lilienthal a few weeks before his death in 1896. It could almost be a report written yesterday.

> The machine was put on the grass and rigged. The 20 foot span wings were covered with a thin, tough, cotton material which was tightly stretched.
>
> The machine was so well rigged that it was impossible to find a single slack bracing cord. The fabric was so tight that the whole machine resonated like a drum when one tapped it lightly.
>
> We climbed to the top of the hill and Lilienthal took his position in the framework and lifted the machine off the ground. He was wearing a flannel shirt and breeches heavily padded at the knees.
>
> I positioned myself well below Lilienthal with my camera and waited anxiously for take off. He faced the wind and took up the position of a runner who was waiting for the starting pistol. At this moment the wind freshened a little; Lilienthal ran three paces forward and as well as leaving the ground went out from the hill almost horizontally. He passed over my head at frightening speed at a height of about 50 feet; the wind made strange noises on the bracing cords of the machine, and it passed me before I was able to direct my camera toward it. Then he glided above the grass skimming the stacks of hay. At about a foot above the ground he shot out his legs forward and landed lightly on the ground.
>
> We sat on the ground and discussed the flight. Grasshoppers clicked on the wing covering. Lilienthal said they were his only passengers and he often heard them jump on the machine when he was in the air.

One of Otto Lilienthal's last flights. He got lift from the bi-wing but he never mastered flight control.

All the objectives that the hang glider pilot wants to attain have already been accomplished by the soaring pilot. The way was a slow, step-by-step progression and the hang gliders are going to take that same path until they achieve their goals. It is interesting to consider that Lilienthal's work led to the glider, but at any point throughout those years when hang gliding lay dormant young people could have picked it up as a sport and developed it. One reason many say it's so popular today is because it is an inexpensive way to fly. That argument would have been just as true all through those quiet years. No, the reason for the great surge to this sport is in some ways an expression of the independence of today's youth. It's not just a great desire to fly, it's a way of expressing an independence in an overcrowded and over-regulated world. Flying with one's face in the wind is a physical and intellectual pleasure. There are not many areas where today's kids can accomplish anything as dramatic as flying entirely by their own efforts. That very feeling may be the Achilles heel that will prevent them from accomplishing the high-performance flight which they seek. They want

These two pictures were taken 80 years apart. A modern-day hang glider and Otto Lilienthal...

to accomplish this with a machine that is a one-man effort. It has to be light, fold up and be carried on top of a car so they can reach an inaccessible area for the launch into excitement. No one can ignore the high accident rate of this sport or the newspaper accounts of communities banning it, but this is not a deterrent. It's estimated that there are seventy-five thousand hang gliding pilots in the world and that figure gets out of date as soon as it's written. Once bitten by this sport, it's like a magical spell.

WHAT KINDS ARE THERE?

There are basically three types of hang gliders: (1) the basic Rogallo wing; (2) rigid aerofoils that are ultra-light and have conventional aircraft construction and control; and (3) the semi-rigid tailless, which can be carried on a car top.

THE ROGALLO

There have been hundreds of variations made on the Rogallo to give it higher performance with improved controllability. Along the way there have been many accidents caused by luffing or collapse of the sail in a dive. Complete control is lost because if the wing is no longer producing a force (lift), the pilot's shifting of weight has nothing to react

... we've gone to the moon but now we're getting back to basics, to flying like a bird.

against. This problem has been solved by a better understanding of the shape of the Rogallo. The basic ninety-degree angle of the leading edge has proven to be safest and the most stable, although its performance is not as good as a wider-swept nose. The cutting of the sail is now understood. The amount of billowing needed is known; that billowing should remain constant from the leading edge to the trailing edge and is now figured carefully into the design.

Making the Rogallo into a higher-performance machine, by increasing the angle of the leading edge and flattening the billow of the sail, is the direction that many of the experts are taking. These gliders should be flown only by experienced pilots.

THE RIGID

The rigid wings, which are of conventional aircraft design, have an 8:1 L/D. That's twice as good as the Rogallo, but rigids have not become popular. Although the Quicksilver, Icarus II and VJ-23 are flown in competition, they are not widely used because they are not one-man machines. They require a trailer for transporting a crew. Actually the rigids are simply ultra-light gliders, with the same controls and with a potential for performance equal to low-performance sailplanes.

Rogallo type.

THE SEMI-RIGID

The semi-rigid is possibly where the future lies. It is collapsible and tailless. Aluminum tubing is used for the leading edge and the spars. Battens or foam produce the airfoil surface and the sail is sleeved on becoming taut and rigid. There are tip draggers or spoilers to help the pilot turn, since weight shifting is not enough. This wing stalls like the conventional glider wing and the luffing problem of the Rogallo is non-existent.

The flight characteristics of the Fledgling, Valkyrie and Easy Rider are different from the Rogallos but basically comprise the same system. The pilot hangs beneath the wind in a harness and shifts his weight against a rigid control brace.

SAFETY

Hang gliding has not had a very good safety record. It would not be fair to any reader not to cover this aspect of the sport. We have stated that one of the attractions of the sport was the sense of personal expression that it provided for a generation of youth that seemed to be all bottled up. Simultaneously with youth's "breaking loose" in the 1960s came the development of the Rogallo wing. With no more than plane designs clipped from magazines and some supplies from the local hardware store they were on the "back forty," crashing at a terrible rate. Lack of knowledge about the air and flight in general contributed much to the

Semi-rigid wing.

Rigid wing with all the controls.

problem. Hang gliding was approached as a Saturday-afternoon lark. Just as the spin was not understood in the early days of aviation, the luffing dive, even for the knowledgeable hang glider pilot, was little understood and created fatalities.

The public asked the FAA to step in and regulate the sport, but the hang gliding community wasn't keen on bureaucratic regulations. Actually, the FAA wanted to stay clear of the whole thing because it knew it wouldn't be able to control the activities of a bunch of kids who were half mountain goat and half bird.

The hang gliders themselves are now doing a good job of educating the public and themselves. They have set up safety procedures and training systems. Hang gliding schools take the student along very slowly, no matter how gung-ho he is.

The improvement and development of the hang glider is now so fast-moving that no one can stay abreast of changes. In the few years since its rebirth, progress has been outstanding. What first started as a way to slide down the side of a meadow on the air instead of the ground has turned into flights to over eight thousand feet, cross-country distances of over thirty miles, and two- to six-hour ridge-soaring flights.

In many ways it's a good thing the FAA did not get in the act or it would have red-taped the pilots out of the sky. But the FAA should be chided for its attitude of turning its head completely aside. It might have been able to save some lives with the structural information it has at its disposal instead of letting the kids find out by hit-or-miss.

Without being attached to the glider by the harness, the student learns to get the "feel" of the wing by running down a gentle incline directly into the wind . . . the wing will lift itself.

There are three parts of any flight: takeoff, flight and landing. There are two ways of talking about these three elements . . . one is theoretical and the other is practical. The problem with the theoretical is that it doesn't do much for the pilot to know that the air is split and travels over and under the wing. That knowledge won't do much for you when you are running down a hill trying to get a thirty-five-pound wing off your back. All the talk about angle of attack won't get lift out of a piece of cloth and a few bars of aluminum. Hang gliding is a sport of feel. For the beginner, the hardest part is the takeoff. It is to be hoped your instructor will have picked a very gentle slope and a wind of about eight miles per hour will be blowing steadily up the slope toward you.

You will not be harnessed into the Rogallo. As you pick up the wing, point it into the wind and run down the hill, you will soon learn all about the theory of angle of attack. If the nose of the kite is too low you will be abruptly stopped as the nose digs into the ground. If the nose is too high it will "dig" into the air and the kite's thirty-five pounds will feel like a hundred. When the nose is pointed correctly, the fabric pops up and forms its twin conical shape and it becomes an efficient airfoil. When done correctly you will be able to run down the hill holding the bottom of the control bar and the hang glider will be weightless in your hands. It takes a lot of strength to fight the wind and dirt, though once done correctly, it is almost an effortless maneuver. But even this first lesson is a thrill. You start with the bar at your waist and, if done properly, the lift of the sail will have your arms over your head and

HOW DO YOU FLY THE CONTRAPTION?

1.

The Rogallo-type wing is the answer for the young and adventurous who want to fly. There is no red tape and it's the cheapest way into the air. Its hanger is the top of a car and in minutes it can be asembled on the edge of a cliff by one man. Turn the page . . .

2.

3.

5.

you'll be running on feet that are feeling half your weight . . . almost flight!

Once this is mastered, the next step is to do the same thing with the harness on and attached to the point of the kite's center of gravity. When you run down the slope you must be standing up straight. Most people have a tendency to lean forward to put their all into the run. This puts the control bar into a position relative to your body so that it can't be maneuvered. The run should be as swift as you can make it and the control bar held ahead of you. The correct pointing of the kite will soon have the fabric accepting the wind and producing lift. It's at this point that the control bar is moved forward ever so slightly. With the nose pointed up, once it is in a lifting configuration it will produce more lift and carry your weight. You will by flying! It may last only a second or two, but it's flight.

Now you are at the stage where heavy clothing will prevent bruised

6.

1.

3.

2.

4. Turn the page for full flight.

The object of hang gliding is to fly like a bird but that shouldn't include nesting in the trees. The pilot was not hurt and the glider only needed minor repairs. The biggest problem was getting it out of the trees. In the top picture you can see that the next pilot flew around the trees . . . not "over" them.

knees and things. Of course a helmet is worn from the start. You will have to practice this feel of the wing over and over so that you can run with it. It's like walking down the street in a very strong wind while carrying a big piece of plywood. If the edge is directed exactly into the wind you can walk. If you go slightly off the wind direction you will be swung around and broadside . . . it will be a board carrying you down the street.

On takeoff, the first few steps should be made with the sail luffing, directly into the wind. A slight push forward will make the wing do its work. The problem is that, as in learning to fly a sailplane, people tend to think they are driving a bulldozer. The feel of the play back and forth on the control bar is something that no one can teach you by telling you . . . it's a feel. You will have a header or two, but remember when you do to let go of the control bar. You are going to fall but don't try to "save" yourself. Fall like a drunk, relaxed. Here is what will happen. If you let go of the control bar as you fall, you will travel forward. The kite has nosed into the ground. It stops instantly. You will go flying through the triangular control bar, but since you are harnessed to the structural members of the glider you will not travel far. It's important that heads, arms, legs and such go on past the bar. Hitting the bar might bend something: you.

The hard part about learning is that you are so close to the ground that there is no maneuvering area. A slight mistake and you are back on earth, which is harder than air. If you were high you could play with the feel and make the flight work, but that chance can't be taken. A good instructor will not allow you to advance up the slope until you can consistently take off, have a flight (even if it's only a few yards) and land standing up. To do that you will have to learn the feel of control. Control comes from the weight of your body. Think of it this way. Make a paper airplane. Throw it across the room; it flies to the far wall. Put a paper clip on its nose; now in flight it will head down; it won't reach the far wall but its flight will be faster. Put the clip near the tail and its initial direction will be up. It'll climb and its flight will be slower than the other two flights. In essence that's what you will be doing when you move the control bar of a hang glider. Remember you are hanging from the center of gravity. In the "neutral" position, the bar is out in front of you, and your flight will be "across the room to the far wall." If you ease the bar back it will be like putting a paper clip on the front of the paper plane. You have pulled the bar back, but what you have really done is pushed your body forward. The nose will head down and you will go faster. If you pull back too far and dive, the nose will hit the dust and you won't be very far behind. If you are in neutral and push the bar away from you, you are putting the paper clip near the tail. If you push the bar too far and stall you will be on your "tail" . . . and so it goes. The whole game is not Bernoulli's theory of forces and counting molecules of air that race over and under the wing and meet at the trailing edge at the same time . . . in fact, most aeronautic experts have given up teaching that theory, but even that is beside the point. Hang gliding is not counting molecules; it is a step-by-step learning process of feeling lift at work.

The turns are made by using body English as well as the movement of the control bar, which shifts the center or gravity. Top left, the pilot banks left. Top right, he's leveled out into straight flight. Right, he's turning right. Unlike a sailplane there is a lapse time of almost a second before the wing responds to the change in shift in the center of gravity.

Turns are made by the same technique—shifting the weight of your body. If you push the bar to the right, in essence you are moving your body to the left. The left wing is forced down and the right wing goes up. The wing that goes up is getting more lift. With more lift it is traveling faster. The faster wing then flies around the lower wing and you are in a turn. Simple? But not so fast. Turns in a hang glider are tricky because you can't allow the down wing to fly too slowly or you will stall it. Like any plane, the flying wing will keep lifting and with a stalled-out lower wing the whole thing will turn over. So, in a turn, the rule is to fly faster . . . the bar comes in slightly (to gain speed) and is pushed to the side (initiating a turn). To slow up after the turn, push the bar forward. Up goes the nose and speed is transferred into a climb.

Well, we are a little ahead of ourselves because you will not be doing turns until you have mastered straight flight. But I saw one group of students learning who never were told the whole story about the control bar. They had a very hard time getting the feel of what they were doing because they didn't understand the whole picture.

To land in an upright, standing position is a matter of judgment. When the flight is about to terminate—that is, the ground is coming up—the flight can end in a nose dive, or the control bar can be shoved forward. The nose will go up, the wing will stall and at zero speed the feet will touch the ground. If the bar is shoved too early, the feet will walk on air . . . not good. If it's shoved too late, they won't be walking. It's all judgment, and that's why it's all done on such a gentle slope that if you misjudge, you won't get hurt.

You will go up the slope ever so slowly . . . yard by yard, and make a longer flight. At some point you will learn about the wing stall. The error will come, but you will not be high enough to get hurt. The technician says the wing has a seventeen-degree angle of flight. That means nothing to a guy flying. The thing that has to be learned is the position of the bar so that the wing keeps its conical shape. Too much up and it can't climb and acts like a brick . . . that is a stall. Too much dive and the sail luffs . . . and at altitude, that is like a dead duck carrying a brick. The luff stall is something they have tried to design out of the Rogallo wing because it takes an act of God to recover from this condition.

The turns in hang gliding have to be learned as carefully as the take-off. The 360 should not be attempted until the pilot is well experienced with straight flight and has completely mastered the 45- and 90-degree turns. Plenty of altitude is needed for the 360 since it's a characteristic of this wing to lose a lot of altitude in the turn. Very shallow turns should be made to start, with enough altitude to recover into straight flight if something starts to feel wrong.

The turns are accomplished with body English, as well as the movement of the control bar. The feet are stuck out in the direction of the turn. The extra weight in that direction, plus the added drag, helps effect the turn. If the turn starts to get too steep, the legs are thrown in the opposite direction. Also, as in soaring, sound will tell you what the wing is doing. The higher the speed the higher the sound level. When things go silent, watch out—a stall is coming.

HANG-GLIDER TURNS

Instrumentation for hang gliders is becoming very sophisticated. This variometer gets attached to the control bar. Not only will it read out the amount of lift or sink but it'll give an audio reading. The pilot hears whether he is in lift or sink and does not have to watch the instrument.

1.

2.

5.

6.

The turn. In picture **1** the pilot is flying along a ridge, and as he moves into the lift he starts to go up, as you can see in picture **2.** He has now risen above the horizon. Obviously he wants to stay in the area of lift, so he starts to turn to fly back to where he had first felt the lift. Note how he makes his turn. It is not only the shift in weight, but you can also see the body English. In picture **3** his legs are thrown out to the left. The added drag helps start the turn. It's continued in picture **4,** but note that the turn has not started. That is the lag time of the turn. In picture **5** the turn starts, and in pictures **6** and **7** he's well into the turn, the drag is reduced and the legs are centered. The turn is held with only the shift in weight, as in picture **8.** Pictures **9** and **10** show that once the wing is in the new direction, the body is centered and the turn continues until the next shift in weight.

136 . . .

3.

4.

7.

8.

9.

10.

1.

2.

5.

6.

9.

10.

3.

4.

7.

8.

This sequence, taken at the regional competition held at Pico ski resort in Vermont, shows how maneuverable hang gliders are. Pilots and their rigs were carried to the top of the mountain in the chair lift. After a 15-minute flight down the mountain there was only one place to land—in the parking lot or in the trees. Only one pilot missed the lot (p. 32). The pilot has all the control he needs, as you can see in this sequence. He brings his wing down through the clearing and makes a perfect landing pattern, ending up heading into the wind, and flairs out for the landing. Turn the page and see the touchdown.

Headed into the wing . . .

. . . the control bar goes forward . . .

. . . the flair-out. The forward speed is almost zero . . .

. . . the "landing gear" is down and a few steps complete the "roll-out."

140 . . .

Cliff launching is the ultimate in this sport. This is for the expert. The trick is to remember you are not flying down a straight visual path that leads to the valley. You must fly directly into the wind, even if it's coming up the slope at an angle. If the wind is over ten miles an hour you could find that the nose on launch is pitched up violently—it could toss you back to where you parked your car. In stiff winds a ground crew will be required to hold the wing at the correct angle to get flight started.

Flying from the altitude of the cliff enables the hang glider to take advantage of all the updraft air currents that the soaring pilot uses. There is no need to repeat them here; they are explained in the Soaring chapter. Ridge soaring is where gliding started and it's the same for hang gliding. The dream is to fly a ridge and get high enough to fly out into the valley, pick up a thermal and circle in it to altitude. The reason the hang glider pilot seeks a wing with high performance is so he can "reach" the thermal and enter it—and not fall out of the sky before having a chance for these dramatic updrafts.

The FAI (Fédération Aeronautique Internationale) has now recognized the hang glider as a sport flying machine and is making determinations about badge awards that are similar to the ones so much coveted in the soaring world. There will be bronze, silver and gold.

A HANGING EXPERIENCE

Not long ago I was the host on a TV show which had been filming in Vermont for four days. The soaring segment had gone well. It was quite a production. The camera crew loved the work. They not only filmed with long lenses from the top of the mountains, but they used chase planes, both motor and sail types. A helicopter was also put into service. As we boarded a charter plane that was to take cast, camera crew, production crew, etc., to Cape Cod for the hang gliding section of the show, the producer took me aside and said, "Now look. You might be a little old to try this hang gliding stuff." Then it was suggested, if I wanted, this segment could be done using my voice-over and letting the expert, Mike Markowski, do the flying. The upshot of that conversation was that next day I was out working under Mike's tutelage to learn how to fly the wing. The crew spent the day wiring the mountain for sound and all the other things that TV crews do. Slowly, ever so slowly, Mike put me through my training. Step by step we worked up the sand dune, getting higher and higher as I demonstrated that I could take off, fly straight and land on my feet.

A launch site about sixty feet up was my first goal. When I was about to try it the cameraman called to me and said, "Why don't you wait twenty minutes and we'll be ready to shoot?" Answering that I'd have time for one practice flight, I put everything I had into the launch.

Standing there at first, looking down, wondering if I was entirely sane, I felt the weight of the control bar digging into my shoulders. Mike's voice interrupted the first state of fear that was about to sweep over me with the command, "Watch the wind sock. Face directly into the wind." My legs must have started because in an instant I felt the wing dig into the air and my legs were churning on nothing. It's hard to

1.

2.

3.

4.

5.

6.

7.

8.

9.

remember anything my body did, but it must have been doing something right. I was flying. But the feeling was remembered. Every inch of the way down that barren dune. A thing of beauty, exhilarating. No other means of flight could be as personal as this. In ballooning it's a calm excitement, in soaring it's calculated, in jumping it's a shock. This was a personal effort with some aluminum and Dacron that produced real flight . . . free flight. It's been reported from in-flight tape recorders that there is one four-letter word that all pilots utter the instant before a fatal crash. If there had been an in-board recorder on my Rogallo, I'm sure it would have recorded the three-letter word that all hang glider pilots must exclaim when they feel flight for the first time: *"Wow!"* I do remember as the ground came up to meet me that I slammed the control bar forward. The wing went up and I was standing ankle-deep in sand. Cheers came up from every member of our team. Better than two hundred yards wasn't bad. I strutted away from the wing feeling a little like Lindbergh in Paris.

The author demonstrates how not to hang-glide. The take-off was fine, as **3** shows a perfect flight starting. In **4** a stall starts, and the weight forward in picture **5** doesn't help things. It looks as though the flight is going better in picture **6,** but actually it takes too long to recover from the stall, and in picture **7** the mistake is compounded. The forward push on the control bar makes the stall worse, and up comes the ground, which fortunately is sand.

The flight down was easy. The climb up was backbreaking, carrying thirty-five pounds of sail that seemed able to choose the exact instant you were off balance to fill up and decide to fly. Everyone praised the "old" pilot at such a fantastic first flight. I shrugged off my success quietly as one would do while having an Olympic gold medal hung around his neck. The director asked again if it wouldn't be better to let Mike fly. I answered that this sport was a piece of cake. Cameras were ready, sound was ready and I was given the signal. I took a last look at the wind sock and raced for the edge of the world.

Again, it is hard to remember anything my body did, but it must have been doing something awfully wrong. Every inch of the way down that barren dune, without flight, I saw every grain of sand. The feeling was remembered. The third letter of the dying pilot's four-letter word was on my lips as flight ceased abruptly. With aluminum, Dacron and nylon harness in disarray I counted parts: two arms...two legs...two heads...one body. All was more or less okay. I heard someone call frantically, "Did you get it?" A cameraman returned, "You bet!"

National television loved that take!

But the show must go on, so old Pagliacci climbed up the hill and with tears in his eyes jumped off the bloody cliff. A fine flight was made, and then I hung up my hang glider.

About a year later I got a phone call asking if I'd like to go to Liechtenstein to do some hang gliding. Knowing it was one of the great areas of the world for this sport, I jumped at the chance. Possibly the word "jumped" is misused in this context.

Liechtenstein was first built by God and then the Romans, and I'm sure they had the hang glider in mind. It's about the size of New York City. About where the Bronx is, is the top of the Alps. Battery Park, in lower Manhattan, is where the Rhine River makes the border between Liechtenstein and Switzerland. You can literally hang glide across the country.

The principality of Liechtenstein has no border guards, no army, no navy and the nearest thing they have to an air force is a ski instructor, Sepp Ender, who teaches hang gliding after the snow is gone. It was the Romans who first started making Sepp's job easy. They built roads that wind crazily from the capital city of Vaduz in the valley up to the village of Malbun, so high that only ten people live there all year round. Any nice day, scores of hang gliders are out climbing to the top of the country in cars with their kites atop. They choose the appropriate road according to the wind. Launching places are to be found any place you can find to park the car off the narrow road.

A group of us took our daily lessons from Sepp and in some ways I got my winged nerves back in some sort of order, but I went there to shoot one picture. Prince Franz Josef II lives in a Walt Disney–like medieval castle that sits high on the cliffs above the capital. I wanted a picture of this fairyland palace taken from a hang glider. Even after a week of intensive training I was not ready to make such a flight. I rigged a motor drive Nikon on the wing, clamped a Zona radio control next to it and told Sepp to jump. He did.

From my safe distance (safe on the ground) I shot him flying over the palace with a long lens and simultaneously pushed the button on the radio transmitter that I held as he flew. When he passed over the city, I raced down to the river by car and retrieved the Liechtenstein air force. Incidentally, Sepp has flown the mail down from the high country and on one festive occasion had tied four bottles of the prince's best champagne (one on each tip of his hang glider) and delivered them to the princely garden for a party. This is to prove that they were wrong in 1903 when they said that flying was for the foolhardy and there was no commercial advantage in aviation, and wrong again in 1970 when they said that hang gliding is only something that crazy kids do to upset their parents . . . Sepp Ender is sixty years old.

The Federal Aviation Administration has many suggestions on how to handle this sport in a safe manner, but they have no specific regulations to govern the sport. Basically, they refuse to recognize the hang glider as a flying machine in spite of the fact that by their own definition of an aircraft and the performance of the hang glider they should be regulating this sport just as they do ballooning, soaring and parachuting. Without these regulations the individual is free to try hang gliding in any matter or means that meets his fancy. Hang gliders can be constructed of any materials, in any design, and flown without training or supervision. This is foolhardy and has proven very dangerous. Accident and death statistics are not complete because there is no governmental agency collecting all the figures, but the figures that are available show that it all started out as an extremely dangerous sport. As training schools have come into being, as manufacturers have stressed safety and as the U.S. Hang Gliding Association has come on the scene to police as much as they can, the accident rate has declined.

This is not a sport to be learned from books, to be tried with a hang glider harnessed on one's back and a magazine article on how to fly in the hand. Like all other flying, this sport must be learned from experienced pilots. Throughout the country there are hundreds of training schools where the student can be sure he is using safe equipment made with aviation-quality materials. The training will be tailored to the progress of the student and in that way keep the person out of trouble. One of the first considerations is whether you are physically fit for this very demanding sport . . . not so much the flying as the lugging of a kite back up the hill. It weighs only about thirty-five to forty-five pounds, but it's difficult to handle in only a little wind.

Classes run about fifty dollars a day with everything included. Some schools have courses that last two or three days. You should receive a ground course, an orientation into every phase and problem of the sport. The first jumps will be supervised and progress should be made in small gradations. Overconfidence is where problems start. Some schools use radio equipment built into the helmet they provide.

YOU SHOULD KNOW . . .
IF YOU ARE GOING TO TAKE UP
HANG GLIDING

Hang-glider flights can be of long duration and spectacular. The same conditions are needed in both hang gliding and soaring. The most common flying condition for hang gliding is ridge lift. You can stay in the air as long as the wind blows. In this set of pictures the pilot will fly across the whole country of Liechtenstein, from the top of the Alps down to the Rhone River. The flight will take about 20 minutes if it's a straight glide. On good wind days you can fly the face of the Alps all day.

The landscape of Liechtenstein is steep and handsome. It's one of the best sites in Europe for the sport. Top left, the pilot surveys his wind problems. The peaks across the river are Switzerland. The take-off and flight are sheer beauty. The thrill is to have controlled flight while hanging out there in the wind . . . just like a bird. Top flying pictures on these pages were taken with a remote-control camera on the wing tip which was fired by a Zona radio from the ground. The bottom picture was taken from the ground with a long telephoto lens as the pilot flew over the Prince's palace at Vaduz. Turn the page and see what the pilot saw with a wide-angle lens at the same time that this picture from the ground was taken.

This enables the instructor to give you guidance all the way through the flight. Some schools use a tandem hang glider so that the instructor actually flies along with the student until he is sure the student can do it himself.

A few good rules: Don't buy a kite until you have consulted with an expert. Keep the ship in perfect repair. Don't make repairs out of makeshift materials. Pre-flight the ship and make certain that it has been assembled correctly...this has been a big factor in accidents. Wear a good quality helmet. Gloves and a simple coverall are good accessories. Don't fly if the wind is over ten to twelve miles per hour and don't do it if you are tired. Do not make turns until your instructor tells you to try them. Make sure the flight path is clear and that there are no power lines. Since dunes close to the ocean are often used as launch sites, beginners should be instructed in quick release from the harness and flotation gear should be worn.

It is advisable not to purchase a hang glider until you are sure whether you want a ridged or nonridged one. You should fly a hang glider that matches your ability and to determine that will take time and experience—especially to get into the high-performance wings.

The art of this sport is changing so fast that the monthly publications should be followed. *Hang Gliding* is the official publication of the U.S. Hang Gliding Association. You should become a member of this organization. This periodical is informative and keeps up to date on the latest trends. USHGA's address is P.O. Box 66306, Los Angeles, California 90066. Other good magazines are *Hang Glider,* a weekly, P.O. Box 1860, Santa Monica, California 90406; *Delta Kite Flyer News,* Van Nuys, California; and *Glider Rider* Newsletter, Chattanooga, Tennessee.

The USHGA can supply a list of all the manufacturers of hang gliders in the country. They will also be able to supply the names and addresses of the schools, clubs and organizations, and sources for materials that will be of aviation standards.

The books in this field are coming along so fast that it's hard to keep up with them. Rick Carrier's *The Complete Book of Sky Sailing*, published by McGraw-Hill, is one of the early ones in the field and very good. It's easy to follow and well illustrated. *Hang Gliding, the Basic Handbook of Skysurfing*, by Dan Poynter, published by Daniel Poynter, Quincy, Massachusetts, is regarded by many as the bible in this sport. Also good is *True Flight* by Herman Rice, Aviation Book Company, Glendale, California. *The Complete Guide to Hang Gliding* by Ross R. Olney, Berkley Publishing, is a good, inexpensive, informative, introductory book to the sport.

5
PARACHUTING

The concept of the parachute was known as far back as the fifteenth century. Sketches of a conical parachute even preceded Leonardo's pyramid idea. The square parachute of Faustio Veranzio became quite well known after the publication of his book in 1615. No other designs appear until the eighteenth century. In 1783, Sebastian Lenormond jumped off a tower in France using long folds of cloth, but that's about all we know about him and his chute. In 1797 the first true parachute jump was made in Paris by André-Jacques Garnerin. He ascended in a balloon to three thousand feet and simply jumped out. The popularity of the sport quickly spread throughout Europe. The "half-grapefruit" was a visible mechanism for descending from great heights. It eventually got to America, and in 1914 a twenty-one-year-old girl named "Tiny" Broadwick made the first free-fall (delayed opening) jump from a plane.

In the chronological order of events, this chapter on parachuting belongs after the ballooning and before the soaring chapter. Why, then, is this chapter on jumping and skydiving last? If the answer is not obvious, I'll tell you straight out. For each of these silent sports I've added my personal feelings and experience with the sport. If I were to write this chapter the same way I'd written all the rest, it would mean I'd have to jump. As the book proceeded to its conclusion, it became time for a little introspection.

When the subject of parachuting comes up in a general conversation, most people emphatically say, "No way." But most people say that about anything they don't understand. I got the same kind of answer when I talked about ballooning or soaring. "You wouldn't get me up in one of those things without a motor! No way!" All the talk about its being safer in a balloon or a sailplane than it is on the road driving to the airport has no effect on them. In some ways they are right. The old argument that more people are killed in bathtub falls than parachuting only means either that skydivers don't take baths or that more people take baths than jump. Although I can't stand on the edge of a building and look down, heights in balloons, sailplanes or hang gliders never bothered me. But—and this is an important but—we are born into this world with two innate fears, the psychologists say. One is the fear of loud noises and the other is the fear of falling. We are trained by life itself to overcome the loud-noise fear, but we do not get much of a chance to overcome the fear of falling. Most of us live with it all our lives. The psychoanalysts tell us that most insecurity dreams include a falling episode. So we are dealing with something that is deeper within us than a dislike for, say, spinach.

One thing my flying taught me: Fear dissipates with knowledge. But then again that is not a general rule. There are some things that make us fearful as our knowledge increases. A child has no fear of running out into the street, but through experience he learns not to do it for fear of being hit. So we can now say that we have two kinds of fear—those real fears we have learned from experience and those things we fear because we have no experience or knowledge about them.

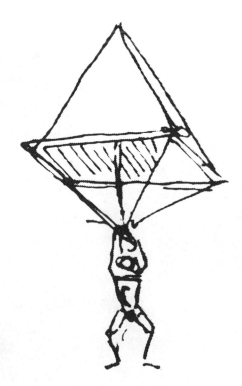

Leonardo da Vinci's notebook on flying machines contained the first parachute design, but it wasn't tried.

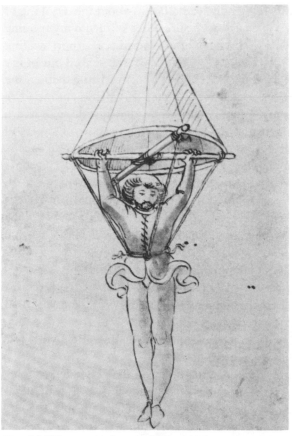

About 1480 a conical parachute was drawn by an unknown designer. There is no record as to whether it was tried.

The italian Veranzio in his book 1615–16 came up with a sail-derived parachute which was known as Veranzio's square.

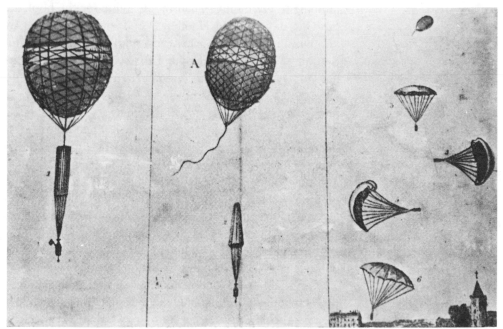

The first-known successful parachute jump was made by André-Jacques Garnerin in Paris on October 22, 1797. The parachute was carried aloft by a balloon and then released, as shown in the step-by-step drawing.

The day I took my first glider flight I had fears about the day I might have to solo. The day I soloed I was so sure of myself from my training that the tension I felt was from standing around at the airport waiting for my instructor to say, "Go do it." Then I became scared out of my wits every morning before a soaring competition. As I rolled down the runway on takeoff I was as cool as a cucumber. Flying taught me to be cool in tight spots. A few months ago while driving alone I had a serious car accident. A drunk came down on my side of the road straight at me. I had no way to turn out of his path. He had an escape route and I saw it, but his headlights kept coming at me. I literally counted down my alternatives and his. When I saw he had no more alternatives I swung the passenger side of my car into his front end. It saved my life and my heart never skipped a beat, nor at any point did I panic. Making decisions one step at a time becomes a pilot's way of thinking.

There is one thing about jumping that is different from any other active sport. Once you pursue a sport and get into trouble—be it motorcycling, skiing, scuba diving, you name it—you have to deal with that problem as it unfolds. There is no stepping back and trying it again. The problem as you find it is ahead of you and you must deal with it as it is. In jumping you have a second chance.

Once I worked all this thinking out I realized that I needed training and knowledge before I could make a real decision as to whether I would be able to jump and I became very curious about how I would respond to the jumpmaster's command, "On the step and go!"

I'm going to tell you all about this, hoping you will try to put yourself in my shoes, or I should say jump boots, and see if you can relate to it. But I had one more problem. It took weeks to broach the subject of jumping to my family. Then the deadline for the book started to creep up. One day I called Hadden Wood, one of the best instructors and jumpmasters in the business, and said, "Do you want to jump me this Saturday?" I'd known Hadden for years. He packed the chute that I had to wear in soaring competition, and I knew his history. He suggested I come to his house on Friday night to talk. I put down the phone and sat thinking out all the answers I'd prepared for the family. After all, I was fifty-seven, a grandfather and all the rest of it. I took a deep breath and made the plunge into the living room, blurting, "I'm going to jump at Stormville Airport with Hadden on Saturday.... Now don't get upset ... it's perfectly safe ... Hadden's a master ... I'll be on a static line ... that's about as ..." And that's about as far as I got. All the jabber that I was getting from my wife and daughter finally filtered through my best arguments. Wife was saying in her quiet way, "I'd like to do it, too." And daughter was screaming, "You can't do it without me!" I stood openmouthed. Did they want to die with me?

Next day, the doctor ruled my wife out on a previous medical problem, but a young friend who was nearly half my age said he wanted to try. Walter was a good sportsman, with lots of nerve. We'd skied together and he's one of those boomers. We'd climbed in the Alps together and we both had done the bobsled run at St. Moritz.

Today the very maneuverable and reliable Para-commander is used at most schools. It is the best there is to learn with. The principal advantage lies in its fast forward glide, about 15 miles per hour, its quick turning response and its slow rate of descent, about 15 feet per second with a 170-pound jumper. Not so long ago this chute was used only by expert jumpers. It costs more than the military-surplus gear, but the rate of descent is one-third less. It's much easier on the beginner.

The most advanced chute is the square ram air, which is derived from the kite designed by Jalbert. It's like the cross-section of an aircraft wing except that it's constructed in cloth instead of aluminum. Early parachutes depended on the drogue effect to bring the jumper down safely. The Para-commander introduced a certain amount of lift in its design. The ram air chutes depend mainly on their lifting function. They can do a forward speed of about 30 miles per hour. They can be flaired out on landing just like a small plane or a hang glider, and touchdown can be as gentle as a tiptoe. They are extremely maneuverable and easy to pack.

Gretchen, age twenty-two, cute as a button, who has had no air experience—her sport was tennis—was high as a kite and couldn't wait for the weekend to get started, but she oscillated between excitement of the coming event and fear of what she might or might not do. We were a perfect threesome because among us we had every possible problem that you will face.

On the way to the airport, all three of us were giddy and things that weren't funny brought mountains of laughter. We were trying to help each other not to think. Then disaster struck; the car radio blurted out Beethoven's *Funeral March*. That quieted our trio. I switched to another station to lighten things up . . . Gracious, do I hate that new music! Hadden met us at the airport and started our six-hour training over a cup of coffee. Everything we learned—and it was a lot, which I'll tell you about—could only be related to that moment of that first jump. As the hours went on we joked about the sweaty palms, and every break period became more serious as each of us was asking way down deep, "Why am I doing this to myself?"

The training can be divided into two categories: those things you want to hear and those you don't. On the don'ts I could see my team sagging a little and taking deep breaths; on the do's they were alert and asking good questions. How to protect your main arteries in a tree

The author tries his hand.

Walter and Gretchen look a little stunned before their first jump. Then they tell their own story.

landing was part of the grueling stuff. Hadden kept saying he wasn't trying to scare us, but such things had to be explained. When he described our equipment I could see that we all were heaving a sigh of relief. We were to use all the latest equipment, including paracommander chutes, which would give us easy landings. We were even going to have radio receivers strapped on our gear and would be talked the whole way down to the ground.

A lot of information was thrown at us in the six hours of training and it's a struggle pounding it into your head. We will go step by step with you as you read on, but at this point, you as a reader and we as students have burning questions: "Will I do it, and how will I react?"

By mid-afternoon we were dressed for the occasion—high boots and jumpsuits—and as our jumpmaster put us in our chutes every part of it was again explained. With the helmet on I felt about as flexible as a straightback chair. How, with all this gear on, could I perform the Parachute Landing Fall (PLF) or arch my back, the first step in the descent?

The walk to the plane brought to mind the old movie *The Last Mile*. The scene is set for the hero—I think it was Paul Muni—as he walks to the electric chair and all the guys in the cells along the corridor are wishing him good luck. Along our path all the experienced jumpers were greeting us with thumbs up and encouraging "good luck!"

At the plane Hadden had us each sit in the doorway and go through our exit procedure. We were given our jump order and loaded into the plane. Five bodies wearing forty pounds of gear in a plane that seats four dressed in street clothes was a feat in itself. As the engine kicked over I saw Gretchen's eyes open wide as she took a deep breath.

Whether you are twenty-two, thirty-three or fifty-seven, the next few minutes of time are going to pass. They are going to be a big personal test, and you feel this very keenly. Which of the three of us will *you* be?

Walter was first. The altimeter strapped on the top of our reserve chute was reading twenty-eight hundred feet. The plane was leveled off. From my position, facing backward with my back against the pilot's seat, I couldn't see Walter as we made our climb to altitude. Walter had never been in a plane smaller than a transcontinental jet. It never dawned on me that this would be a problem for him. The door was opened and, on the command from Hadden, Walter swung his legs out and put them on the step. His hands reached out for the wing strut. Then came the command, "On the step and go!" Walter's hands slipped further out on the strut and he was standing on the step. It seemed like an eternity. It was. The little plane, with power cut to reduce the prop wash, droned on. Walter froze. His clothes flapped, but he was solid. Then he slipped his hands back down the strut, swung around and was back sitting in the plane.

"My God," I thought, "how will I do?" I've seen Walter take a whole Swiss Alp in one swoop on skis. I've seen him gingerly work his way up a ninety-degree rock face with only the sole of one boot between him and a glacier three thousand feet below. The famous

Gretchen actually was a good student. Her instructor talked very quietly to her. She followed his instructions in spite of the fact that she was so scared that she was almost sick. She got on the step, stretched and went. Her arch was good, and even her PLF landing was good. She couldn't wait for the next weekend to go again.

bobsled run at St. Moritz was a frolic for him. For only a moment I saw Walter's face. It showed fear.

The door was closed and the little Cessna's engine was purring again, so I couldn't hear what Hadden was saying to Walter. We banked and in a few minutes the door was opened again and before I could turn and get into position to see, Walter was already on the step and I caught a glimpse of him hurtling through space. I heard the static line hit the plane and Hadden was leaning out, watching what I knew was a good descent by the relaxed position of his body. Then he turned to the pilot and I could read his lips as he said, "Fine." His own account of the jump follows.

Walter:

The pilot cut the engine to idle speed. I was now sitting in the open door. Hadden, my jumpmaster, shouted, "On the step!" I climbed slowly out to my place under the wing. The air hit me; I looked down twenty-eight hundred feet and saw the airport. "Go!" Hadden yelled. I looked down again and suddenly I was scared. I chickened out. . . . I just couldn't do it. I climbed into the plane again. Hadden talked to me and reassured me that I was able to do it . . . I shouldn't worry. "Well?! Okay, let's try it again!" I said.

I moved into the ready position as we circled, and then Hadden told me to get onto the step again. The engine was cut. It felt as though the plane tipped and I climbed out. This time I just had to do it. I knew if I didn't go I'd be disappointed in myself. Hadden yelled, "Go!" I let loose with my hands, sidestepped and tried an arch. I counted, "Arch thousand," but then a new feeling took me for the next few seconds. There was no sensation of falling, of wind, noise or speed. I had no idea which way was up, down or sideways. I must have tumbled, I think! I don't know how long it took the static line to do its work. When the chute did open, there wasn't the wrenching I had expected; in fact, it was almost gentle. When I felt myself hanging, I looked up and saw a beautiful chute with the sun shining through the colored panels. Then I looked down and it was just incredible. I was dangling here at two thousand feet. That was another complete rush: it felt like being clutched in my girlfriend's arms. I floated and laughed out loud and my imagination went crazy.

What a rush! What a high! I was yanked out of my euphoria by the transmitter's blurting something about my having a good canopy and that I should pull slightly on my right toggle. The target area below me was growing larger and getting closer. I went over the basics of the Parachute Landing Fall (PLF) technique for myself and started to put my feet and knees together, looking at the horizon. Everything was coming up faster and faster. Then I hit and rolled with forward speed. Surprisingly, the PLF worked very smoothly. There was no more bump to it than jumping off a stepladder. I got up and ran downwind of my chute, which was collapsing on itself in the grass. Then there were congratulations all around. It was without a doubt one of the greatest feelings I've ever experienced in my life. It's one of the most exciting sports around. Scared?! You bet, but there's something about falling through the sky that makes it all worthwhile. And the experience stays with you and you're at a mental high for hours after the jump.

Gretchen was another story. She was as different from Walter as night is from day. She was scrunched in the back of the plane facing forward. She could not see out because she is so small. At first glance, she looked like a pile of khaki rags in the corner. At about one thousand feet up I saw her close her eyes. Her head wobbled and when she opened her eyes she was looking at me. I smiled at her, but got no smile in return. I watched her closely. Her face turned the color of the rags. She opened her eyes and I read her lips, "I think I'm getting sick. Don't think I can do it." I leaned forward and patted her on the leg, shook my head and said to her that it was okay and not to do it. Everything was okay. She closed her eyes. Stupidly I had forgotten that no one should be in a small plane with closed eyes if airsick. Watching the horizon will prevent airsickness in many cases. When Walter had his problem Gretchen almost lost her cookies, but I saw that when the door was opened the color came back to her sick but pretty face. As soon as Walter had jumped I whispered to Hadden, "Gretchen might be too sick." His back had been to her the whole time and he hadn't seen her problem. He immediately opened the door to give her plenty of air, then signaled to me that he would handle it.

"Okay, Gretchen," he said in a cheerful manner, "you're next."

The air seemed to do wonders for her cheeks. I gave her leg a good-luck squeeze as she maneuvered herself toward the door. Hadden talked to her for a moment as the plane leveled off. He signaled for the engine to cut and on the command, "On the step and go!" Gretchen moved with the agility of a well-schooled athlete . . . the foot out into space . . . the stretch . . . and she was away.

I yanked my head around. Out of the corner of the window I saw her open chute floating away. What guts!

Gretchen:

I guess it was not being able to see out of the plane (along with the fear of falling twenty-eight hundred feet to the ground) that upset my stomach so badly. I needed air to ease the nausea. My palms were clammy and cold but my face was hot. My head ached. What the hell was I doing up here? How stupid to spend all that money for this stunt! Fresh air, please! It's not real. Ignore it . . . ignore everything. The open door! Fresh air! Poor Walter. Open the door. "Gretchen, stand by" . . . fresh air . . . great . . . "On the step and go" . . . fresh air!

I remembered to arch when I let go but not much more. I must have steered the landing pattern right because I landed at the right spot. I must have automatically assumed the PLF position because the landing was so easy I don't remember it. Oh, but I remember the ground. For days I had grass stains under my fingernails. It was great. Great. I can't wait for my second jump.

I was next. I had a tremendous advantage over the rest of my team. I'd been in the air in everything that doesn't have a motor. Seeing things down there at three thousand or twenty-five thousand feet doesn't bother me. But when Hadden motioned me to the jump seat place, my palms were wet. I went over in my mind the four counts he'd taught us. Then I pushed that out of my mind. I checked to see that my static line was hooked to the pilot's seat, although I'd watched Hadden do it. I was not cool, but I was in no way upset. I waited for his command "Get ready." I swung my feet out and now remember that I thought the load on my body was terribly awkward. On command I stepped out . . . stretched with my right arm up the strut . . . dangled my right foot and was away arching (I hoped). I counted and on two looked for the ring and on three pulled. Somewhere in there I felt a tug. I knew the chute opened and forgot to look up to see if in fact it had. Instantly a voice from my pocket radio said, "Number three, you have a good canopy." There was at no time the sensation of falling. I reached up to find the steering toggles. The voice said to pull on the right toggle. I did and turned 180 degrees instantly. I became fascinated with the steering mechanism and tested both sides. I swung around like a yo-yo. The voice said, "Number three, I'll tell you what toggles to pull." Then I noted the fantastic fall scenery and tuned that out as quickly. I liked the floating sensation and that fast tuned out. I remember thinking that the scary part, the step off the plane, was over; I had a good open canopy; I needed no emergency procedures; my flight, direction and landing pattern were being handled by an all-business voice from the ground. One more problem ahead . . . the landing. Hadden had said that if we got into the right position to have our body absorb the impact we wouldn't get hurt. He also said that the landing happened so fast that you could not command your body to fall one way or the other. The whole thing was body position in preparation for impact. I practiced that position all the way down . . . the hell with the beautiful scenery. Legs together was the command over the radio. I hit Mother Earth facing directly into the wind. I banged my head in my roll, but the helmet did its job. With the chute still open I was dragged. The calm voice said, "Pull in on one set of lines." The chute collapsed and that fast I realized I'd done it! That is the moment of truth for the beginner.

I spotted Gretchen running to me. She was as excited as a puppy. I grabbed her and gave her a hug that I really meant. She bubbled with her own excitement. I was overwhelmed by her joy and was so proud of her. Walter ran over and we all hugged.

Gretchen then said a nice thing. "We've done it! It makes me feel so close to you both."

TRAINING TO JUMP

If you can get to the point of saying, "I'll go to a jumping center and listen to what they have to say," you'll jump. You are coming to this sport at a time when all the development problems have been worked out. Like hang gliding, you are on your own, with no instructor in the "back seat," but unlike hang gliding the equipment is very sophisticated and very close to its ultimate design. The more advanced training centers start the student in a high-performance chute from the very beginning. The surplus military chute is not used at these centers, because it starts the student off at a real disadvantage. The Paracommander is the most popular and best chute money can buy. It has a forward glide speed of

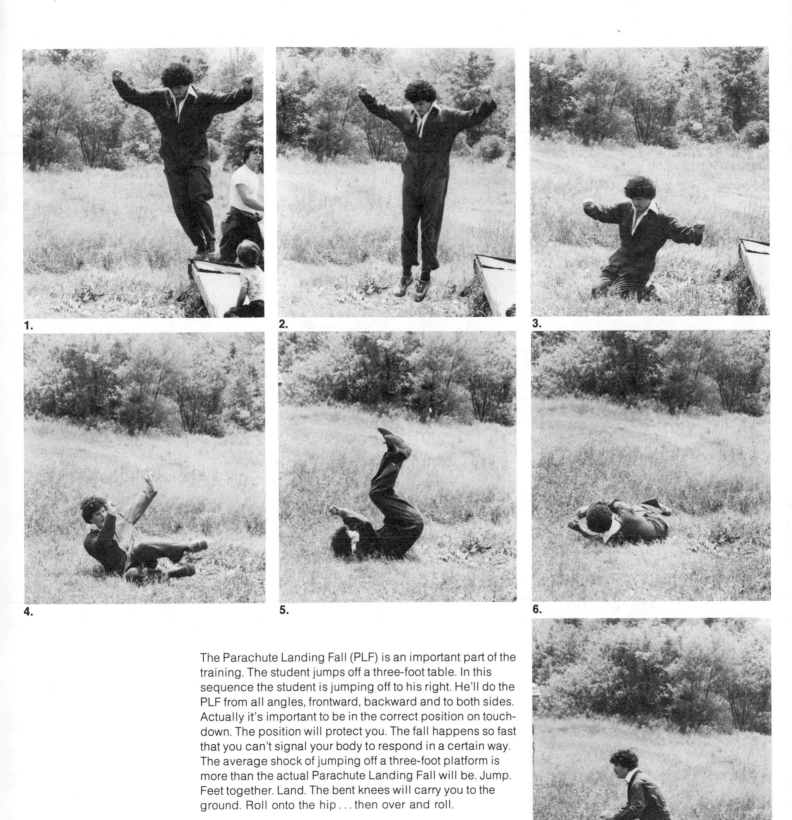

1.

2.

3.

4.

5.

6.

The Parachute Landing Fall (PLF) is an important part of the training. The student jumps off a three-foot table. In this sequence the student is jumping off to his right. He'll do the PLF from all angles, frontward, backward and to both sides. Actually it's important to be in the correct position on touchdown. The position will protect you. The fall happens so fast that you can't signal your body to respond in a certain way. The average shock of jumping off a three-foot platform is more than the actual Parachute Landing Fall will be. Jump. Feet together. Land. The bent knees will carry you to the ground. Roll onto the hip . . . then over and roll.

7.

The instructor gives the student as much of a feel of what is going to happen and what his job will be in and around the Cessna 182. **1** The first command from the instructor is "Stand by!" The student moves into the doorway and sits with his feet on the jump step. **2** The next command is "On the step and go!" The jumper stands on the step, facing forward. His left leg takes all his weight. He's holding onto the wind strut. He moves his right arm out toward the wing tip. His right leg is dangling in space. Then he steps off as in picture **3**. **4** As the jumper leaves the step he will be in an arched position. With his arms, legs and back in the arch, his

1.

4.

5.

body will fall flat, belly down. The student starts his counting sequence. "Arch, one thousand!" **5** "Look, two thousand!" is the next count. The student puts his right hand on the rip cord and looks at it to see that he really has it. The left hand is brought back to balance the amount of air striking him, or he'd start to rotate. **6** "Pull, three thousand!" he shouts to the world as he pulls on the imaginary rip cord and assumes the arch position. **7** "Look, four thousand!" Here the jumper looks over his shoulder to see if the canopy is starting to release. At the end of this count, then he will have to go into his reserve procedures. Different schools may have different systems of counting, but they all add up to the same thing.

about fifteen miles per hour and a rate of descent, about fifteen feet per second, that is roughly one-third slower than the military chutes. The fast forward glide, quick turning response and slow rate of sink make it much easier for the beginner. The standard parachute is just a drag surface; the PC is a crude airfoil that develops lift as it glides forward. It'll take about five to eight hours to hear all the information your instructor will have for you. You will feel very confident about the equipment and in the first jumps practically all the work will be done for you. Your first jumps will be by static line. An eight- to twelve-foot cord attached to the plane will open your chute for you. You must learn to exit properly.

There are a couple of ways to exit a plane, but no matter which one is used the result has to be the same. The body must be in an arched position from head to toe.

In the arched position the body will fall in a very stable manner, belly first. The most common error is bending forward at the waist. This results in an out-of-shape tumble. The chute will still be opened by the static line, but there is no telling what position you will be in

2.

3.

6.

7.

when it does. You will practice all of this on the ground, but here is what it adds up to.

You will be sitting on the floor of the plane as it climbs to altitude. The jumpmaster will open the door and drop a weighted roll of orange crepe paper out as the plane first passes the target area. He will get the wind drift factor by watching how far it lands downwind of the drop zone (DZ). Then the pilot will go around again. You'll be commanded to jump upwind of the DZ the same distance that the crepe paper went downwind. If the wind does not shift or change in velocity you'll drift to the DZ. While sitting and then scooting into position inside the plane, you should always remember to keep your hand over your D-rings on the reverse chute. A free parachute inside the plane can be a very dangerous thing.

You will be moved to the door. Your back will face the engine; the static line will be attached to the plane, usually the pilot's seat. You should check to see that this is done. Keep your left hand over the rip-cord of your reserve chute. As you approach the drop zone the jump-

HERE'S WHAT HAPPENS

Turn the page to see how one of these students made out on his first jump.

1. The command is "Stand by!" The student sits in the doorway with legs on the step.

3. The jumper reaches to the right with his arm and leg, and off the step he goes.

2. The command is "On the step and *go!*" The camera is started and running at five frames a second.

4. This position should put him in an arched fall, belly first. Turn the page.

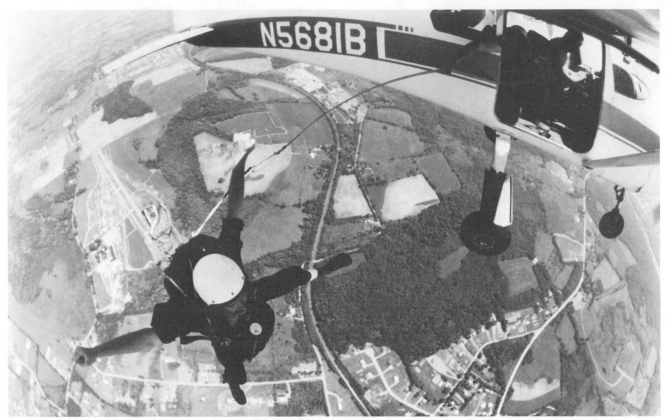

5. He goes through his counting. "Arch, one thousand!" He's feet first...

6. ... but he's remembering to go through with his count. "Look, two thousand!"

7. It takes only a few seconds before the chute starts to open. His landing will be on the airport.

master will command you to get ready. You will swing your legs out onto the step with your knees together, facing forward about forty-five degrees.

On the command "On the step and go!" you should lean forward, reach for the strut and pull yourself out. The engine will have been cut so the air stream will not be too uncomfortable; in fact you won't even notice it. With all the weight on the left foot, the right leg in dangled off into space and the right hand reaches as far to the right as it can go. By dropping off in this position you are already in a stretched-out or arched position. The trick is not to look down . . . look straight ahead.

Once the canopy is opened you should make some observations on the ground so that you will know what is straight ahead of you, because that is the direction from which the wind is blowing. You will be facing into it. That's called the windline. Unlike the sailor, the jumper cannot tell the direction of the wind by what he feels on his face. Let's say the wind is blowing at fifteen miles per hour. If you face into it, it'll feel like fifteen miles per hour coming straight at you. If you turn and face downwind the chute will be traveling at fifteen miles per hour, so it'll feel like the wind is coming from that direction. Actually, with a canopy that flies fifteen miles per hour, facing into a fifteen mile per

STEERING

1. A square ram air parachute is being packed. First it has to be spread out on the ground...

2. ...the canopy is spread out on its side. This whole process will take only about 15 minutes to do.

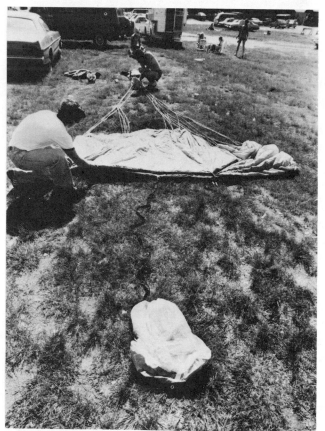

3. The suspension lines are arranged in groups as a helper puts tension on the harness and the packer is starting to fold...

4. ...the envelope into accordion folds. The object in the foreground is the pilot chute.

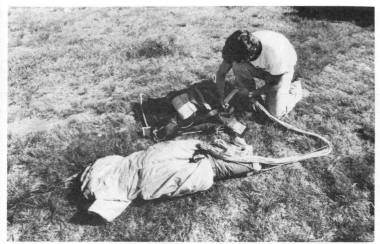

5. The canopy is folded and a "diaper" is put around the skirt to control the opening. The suspension lines are . . .

6. . . . woven into the container, and the canopy itself is folded into the container . . .

7. . . . the container is closed and the only thing remaining is the pilot chute. It has no spring. It's a throw-out type that . . .

8. . . . is packed and attached on his chest. When he wants to deploy the main chute he throws the pilot, which on opening pulls the main.

hour wind will give you a ground speed of zero. With your back to the wind you will be traveling down the windline with a ground speed of thirty miles per hour.

Steering the chute is simple. On each of the rear risers is a wooden toggle. By pulling down on the toggle the canopy will be distorted on that side and caused to rotate. Toggles should be used smoothly; jerking down on them will set up an oscillation.

If you did not turn or tumble during the exit or opening, you will be facing upwind from the target. There are three steering directions that will enable you to land on target.

Steering is a matter of judgment, but you will have help if your training school is well equipped. Our threesome had radio receivers about the size of cigarette packages clipped in our pockets. As soon as we jumped and had the chute open, a voice came over the radio saying, "You have a good canopy." That voice from the ground was very reassuring. All the way to touchdown the voice gave us steering instructions.

The photographer, Pat Rogers, has just left the aircraft on his back, and the jumpers are leaving single file. They are going to hook up, which is called relative work. The first man has to assume a position of resistance. He'll travel at about 125 miles per hour. The last man out must go head first with as little resistance as possible. He'll travel at about 200 miles per hour and catch up with the first jumpers.

The jumpers all caught up with each other. The last to leave the plane dove down and the first held their speed down. They then maneuvered to make this star. This is about to become a 14-man star; they have put them together with over 60 people. All sorts of designs are made—diamonds, squares, pinwheels and things.

Holding means facing into the wind. You will descend with the slowest forward or backward movement over the ground. If the chute will fly at fifteen miles per hour and the wind speed is ten miles per hour, you will have a forward ground speed of five miles per hour.

Running means keeping your back to the wind and to the landmark you noted when the canopy was first opened. With a wind speed of ten miles per hour plus a flying speed of fifteen miles per hour the across-the-ground forward speed will be twenty-five miles per hour. A typical descent on the windline is a combination of running and holding maneuvers to set you over the landing spot.

Crabbing is facing sideways to the wind. It's used when you are off the windline due to an error in spotting or because of a wind shift. You will have both components, holding and running, working at one time. You will be moving toward the windline at about half the speed of running.

THE LANDING

This first-time jumper wrongly thought his main chute had not opened and immediately deployed his reserve chute. He was instructed by radio to pull in the reserve so it would not interfere with his main. He tucked it between his legs for safekeeping.

IF PROBLEMS DEVELOP

The Parachute Landing Fall, commonly called PLF, is a proven method of landing. Your fall is progressively cushioned to a halt. With a chute like the Paracommander the rate of descent will be about fourteen feet per second. This landing can be simulated by a jump from a four-foot table. You might think there is nothing to it, but there is. If you use the PLF you will not get hurt. The hands grasp the risers above your head; the elbows are held close together in front of your face to protect your head. The legs are slightly bent, but not held rigidly. There should be a little tension in the calf and thigh. Your feet, ankles and knees should be touching and you will land flat-footed.

Practice the PLF and roll from a table until you feel comfortable doing it to the right, left and backward. In flight you should concentrate on your PLF body position when you're one hundred feet off the ground. The direction of the roll will be determined by the direction of your drift across the ground. You should not look down to see where the ground is. You will misjudge the landing if you try to step out and meet the ground as it comes up to meet you. You should look at the horizon, assume the PLF position and wait for touchdown. Once you have made contact you will have no more control over the fall. It all happens so fast that there is no way, once your feet have made contact, that you can tell your body to touch knees, next hip, and drop the shoulder for a roll on your back. Actually, if you assume the correct landing position, keeping your eyes on the horizon, legs together, the PLF roll will happen automatically; you will not get hurt and will be amazed at how easy the landing is.

As we have said, this is the only active sport in which, if a problem develops, you have a chance of starting at the beginning with a clean slate; your second chance is the reserve chute. There are a number of theories about how to deploy the reserve chute. At our training center we were told to obey the voice from the ground. Here is what would happen if there was a problem with the main chute. You would be instructed to "cut away." On each shoulder is a release called a Capewell. The new-style Capewells are very simple to use. The thumb and first finger of each hand grab the tabs and both are pulled simultaneously. That simply, the jumper is separated from the problem chute. As our instructor said, "You get that monkey off your back." Now there will be no problem of the reserve's getting tangled in the malfunctioned main chute. But just so the student doesn't panic and forget to pull the reserve ripcord, there is another sophisticated touch called the Stevens connection. It's a connection between the main chute and the reserve. When the Capewells are pulled and the main chute is separated from the harness, the Stevens connection automatically pulls the reserve ripcord. When you are about to pull the Capewells to get rid of the bad chute, you should keep your legs together so that it will be impossible for you to straddle the reserve, which could cause deployment problems. On a chest-pack reserve, your body will be in a backward slant position because of the low suspension point of the chute. On landing you should arch your back slightly and keep your legs together so you will land on your feet, not your fanny. Don't try to cushion your landing with your hand behind you . . . you'll break your arms.

After about five static-line jumps you will be ready to pull the ripcord yourself. Progress seems to be rapid at this point and delayed falls will be started. Different schools have their own systems of making the free-fall longer and longer. The usual method is to start with five-second delays and after about five jumps progress to ten-second delays, and so on.

You will learn the frog position, which is more comfortable to hold than the extreme arch. To do the frog, the back is arched and the arms, legs and neck are relaxed. The arms and knees will be bent and your feet will float upward; your face will be toward the ground. This is not only comfortable but stable and maneuvers can be made from this position.

In the frog position a falling body is a controllable airfoil. Speed can be controlled. In this position the body will fall at 120 miles per hour. From the frog position, turns can be initiated by twisting at the waist and dropping the shoulder forward (toward the ground). To stop the turn you have to turn the other way until rotation stops. You will advance through the loop, barrel roll and/or tracking.

After two hundred or so jumps you will be ready for relative work with other jumpers. You'll be using at least thirty-second delays. Making good clean hookups is precision work. Slamming together or grasping at each other is dangerous. Maneuvering slowly, closing the gap, slowing down or speeding up, turning, are the fine points of the game. This is a world of its own.

All parachuting in the United States is controlled by the Federal Aviation Administration. The FAA regulations, Part 105, Part 149 and Part 65 deal with parachuting and can be obtained from the FAA, 800 Independence Ave., S.W., Washington, D.C. 20591. The U.S. Parachute Association is the organization that represents the public in all jumping activities.

The safety rules require the jumper to wear two chutes, a main and a reserve. The reserve chute must be packed by a licensed rigger. When this chute has not been used for sixty days it must be repacked. Jumps should not be made over populated areas or from an altitude of less than twenty-five hundred feet. Proper boots should be worn, plus helmet and gloves. Flotation gear is required if the jump is to be made within one mile of water. A red flashing light must be worn for night

This is the newest form of relative work. It was not so long ago that jumpers would not consider touching each other's canopies. With the ram air chutes they find there is no danger. Above is the geometric design called canopy stacking. As many as eight jumpers have stacked up. To the right the latest form of relative work is the biplane and in this case the triplane. They have made an eight-man octaplane. They usually start at 10,000 feet and work together. They put their feet in the risers of the man below. You can see how it works with this front view and the side view on the next page.

jumps and oxygen is required for jumps from above fifteen thousand feet.

The cost for the first jump will range from $50 to $75, which will include all the necessary equipment, the ground training course and the plane lift. Succeeding static-line jumps will cost from $12 to $20. Free-fall jumps will cost from $3 to $7.50.

The U.S. Parachute Association (USPA), founded in 1957, is the parent organization. There are over fifteen thousand dues-paying members but many more thousands have had the thrill of parachuting. The USPA promotes and coordinates skydiving activities. They have more than twenty training centers and over two hundred affiliated clubs and drop zones. They publish a monthly magazine, provide public liability insurance, set up safety guidelines and conduct the contests. Write to the U.S. Parachute Association, 806 15th Street, N.W., Washington, D.C. 20591 for a list of training centers in your home area.

Skydiving is one sport where you need not make a large cash outlay for equipment until you decide to pursue the sport seriously. You can usually find a market in used gear at your local club. As the experienced jumpers go for more sophisticated gear, the newcomers can benefit financially. Surplus chutes that are modified for sport jumping are the least expensive way into the game. The Paracommander and the Parafoil are the latest word in advanced jumping technology. The Paracommander has high performance and if possible should be used by the beginner. The Parafoil, with its power to penetrate into the wind, is for the experienced jumper.

The French paraboot is the most popular. It's made by Richard Ponvert in France. It features a pneumatic sole and foam-cushioned ankle support. Do not use mountain-climbing or ski boots for jumping.

Any good helmet will do the job. Gloves should be insulated but not thick, with a gauntlet to cover the wrist. The latest in jumpsuits is not the slick coverall that has reached into fashion design for women but a floppy suit that makes the jumper look like a flying squirrel.

Altimeters come in two forms: those made to be attached to another piece of equipment, such as a chest-pack chute, or to be worn like a wristwatch. The Altimaster is the most popular. It reads up to twelve thousand feet with one hundred-foot marks. It's lightweight, thin and well built.

A real safety feature is the automatic ripcord release. It can be used with either the main or reserve chute. It's made for the armed forces by Guardian Parachute, a division of FXC Corp. Skydivers can set the control to open the chute anywhere between one thousand and three thousand feet above the ground.

As for reading, *Parachutist*, the USPA monthly magazine, is informative and entertaining and is the official publication of the sport. *T.N.T.*, a periodical published in Orange, Massachusetts, is a good source for buying and selling used gear.

Good information is contained in the mail-order catalogues. Some of the larger supply houses are The Chute Shop, P.O. Box 445, Flem-

Para-skiing got its start in Switzerland. It's a combination of parachuting and downhill skiing. There are a number of ways to score the game, but the most common is to start the clock when the jumper hits the ground. He must try to land as close as possible to his skis. Then he puts on his skis and races down the mountain to a finish line. The shortest time wins.

ington, New Jersey 08822; Parachutes Incorporated, 24 N. Main St., Orange, Massachusetts 01364; and Para-Gear Equipment Co., 3839 W. Oakton St., Skokie, Illinois 60076.

Here are some of the more popular books on jumping: *Parachutes and Parachuting* by Bud Sellick, Prentice-Hall, is popular and entertaining and a good look at the whole sport. Dan Poynter's *Parachuting Manual and Log*, published by Parachuting Publications, Santa Barbara, California, is the definitive book on the sport. *Sport Parachuting* by Charles W. Ryan, published by Henry Regnery of Chicago, will appeal to the prospective parachutist. Also good reading are *The Story of Parachuting*, by Don Dwiggins, published by Crowell-Collier Press, London, and Howard Gregory's *Parachuting's Unforgettable Jumps*, published by Pageant-Poseidon, New York.

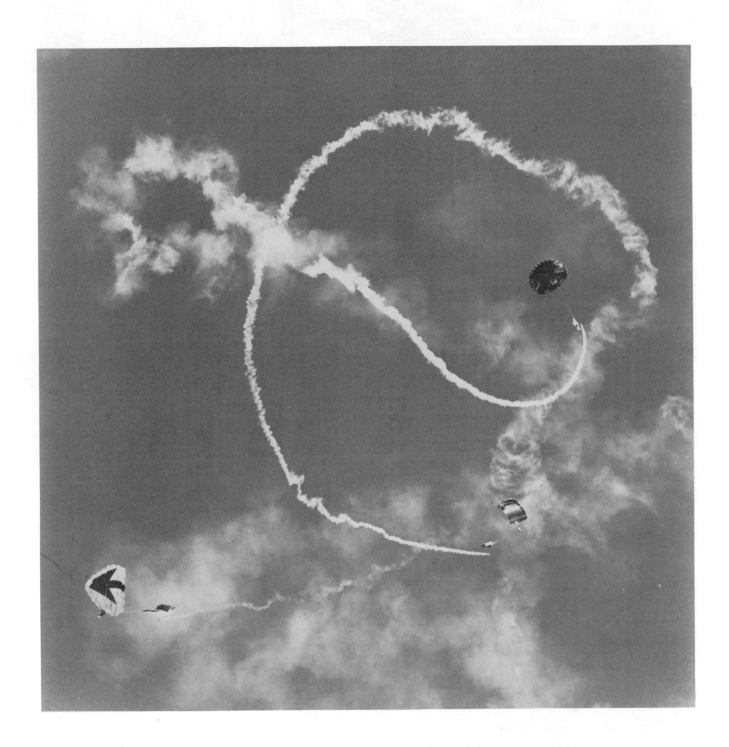

INDEX